Survival Till Seventeen

Leonard Feeney as a Jesuit priest

LEONARD FEENEY

SURVIVAL TILL SEVENTEEN

A Memorial Edition

With an Introduction by S. M. Clare

ST. BEDE'S PUBLICATIONS
Still River, Massachusetts

"Survival Till Seventeen" originally published in
The Leonard Feeney Omnibus by
Sheed & Ward Ltd., London, 1948

Copyright © 1980 by St. Bede's Publications
All Rights Reserved
PRINTED IN THE UNITED STATES OF AMERICA

Imprimi potest: cum permissu superiorum
Societatis Jesu

Nihil obstat: Arthur J. Scanlan, S.T.D.
          Censor Librorum, New York

Imprimatur: +FRANCIS J. SPELLMAN, D.D.
          Archbishop, New York

New York, September 18, 1948

The *Imprimatur* and the *Nihil obstat* are official
declarations that a book or pamphlet is free of
doctrinal and moral error. No implication is contained therein that those who have granted the
Imprimatur and the *Nihil obstat* agree with the
content, opinions, or statements expressed.

LIBRARY OF CONGRESS CATALOGING IN PUBLICATION DATA

Feeney, Leonard, 1897-
    Survival till seventeen.

    Reprinted from the 1948 ed. of author's The Leonard
Feeney omnibus published by Sheed & Ward, New York.

    1. Feeney, Leonard, 1897-   —Biography—Youth.
2. Authors, American—20th century—Biography.
3. Catholic Church—Clergy—Biography. 4. Clergy—
United States—Biography.   I. Mary Clare, Sister, 1925-
II. Title.

PS3511.E17Z478   1980   282'.092'4 [B]   79-25067
ISBN 0-932506-08-9

Contents

To
Father Gabriel Gibbs
and the
Monastic Community of
Saint Benedict Center,
steadfast and loyal
during the difficult years

SMC

Introduction

LEONARD FEENEY was a genius, with the temperament of a genius, intuitive and inspiring, intense and restless, lonely, unpredictable, and complex. Considered a thundering saint by some, a fanatic rebel by others, he was undoubtedly one of the most controversial priests in the history of American Catholicism. Behind his avant-garde originality lay an unswerving fidelity to Tradition; and while he seemed to be against the Establishment, he was at the same time fiercely loyal to the institutional Church.

Courage and greatness appealed to him. Cowardice and mediocrity repelled him. "We can't match God in majesty," he used to say, "we can't match Him in power or wisdom or splendor; but we *can* match Him in love. He gave *all* and we can give *all*. And the little time we have on earth is our chance to give Him all we have, all we do, and all we are." He wanted to give his life in testimony of his faith. Unquestionably he gave up everything else: literary fame, friends, a fine reputation, kudos, accolades and honors. He was incapable of hesitating to act from lack of courage or even from a compromise of courage. Yet nothing could be predicted of his actions with assurance for he was the personification of contradiction and paradox. He was oblivious to physical danger, but afraid of personal criticism. He would cover up with loud, exaggerated complaints of injustice, resorting to sharp, *ad hominem* attacks in prose or verse. These are usually the characteristics of a petty man. But he was not petty nor could his worst critics call him that. Perhaps we could say of him what was said of St. Jerome: "Hard on himself, he showed the same severity toward those who disagreed with him, even very dear former friends.... But everywhere and at all times (he) whose lips let fall so many harsh words, remains a priest whose virtue disarms the most suspicious hatred. Succeeding ages will fondly repeat his wonderful expressions of obedience and devotion to the Holy See. And the Church, despite (his) excesses of language, will place on his brow the halo of the saints."[1]

Leonard Feeney was the epitome of kindness to those he loved. But not to everyone. We can believe him when he wrote, "The Irish are intense, positive, assertive, with an infinite capacity for hatred." They are also inconsistent, sensitive, and scrappy. Quintessentially Irish himself, he could annihilate an enemy with a line, a look, a verse, or a pun. But at the slightest favorable response, he would forget his animosity and accept the same person as his closest friend. He could concede in such cases without losing his authority.

The Catholic Church in America had no better writer and speaker than he, yet he was silenced efficaciously and some of his best-selling books were banned. He reacted with exceptional vigor and showed the explosive possibilities of the Irish temperament when it is combined with genius. Some considered him a brilliant, saintly, courageous, many-faceted, forthright personality not to be fully understood. Others called him rude, unreasonable, proud, despotic, or deranged. But, for a rude, unreasonable despot, he accomplished so much as a writer, religious leader, and reformer that a wise critic will avoid typing him too quickly.

He wrote popular books, lectured at Jesuit colleges, edited

[1]cf. Mourret-Thompson, Vol. 2, pp. 266-267.

poetry for *America* magazine, broadcasted on the "Catholic Hour," and was considered a supreme success. Because he was silenced and "excommunicated" he was considered a catastrophic failure. Yet he was far more effective and far-reaching as a failure than as a success. The years of failure were hard, but from them came the fruition of his suffering: the birth of a new religious community for the Church, with men and women committed to continue what he began, perpetuating his belief that all of man's problems are ultimately theological—an intuitiveness which will survive his academic or literary genius.

I

Leonard Feeney, described by many as "the American G. K. Chesterton," because of the brilliancy of his writings and his wit, has recorded the early years of his life in a series of essays called "Survival Till Seventeen." He begins his biography by calling his birth certificate "such a decisive, laconic, frightening document, that I have often stared at it with something of the feeling one might have if he could tip-toe into his own nursery and find himself asleep in his own crib." This frightening certificate assures us he was born on February 15, 1897, in Lynn, Massachusetts, the child of Thomas Butler Feeney and Delia Agnes (Leonard) Feeney.

Leonard Feeney and Lynn, Massachusetts were made for each other like Nathaniel and Cana or Peter and Bethsaida. In a small town it is easy to be educated in "the hard school of wonder." "Spontaneous drama rose out of the dullness of the environment and the versatility of our own invention," he said.

He idolized his mother, a gentle, exquisite lady, simple and untutored, who married at seventeen and bore him, her firstborn of four, at eighteen. He was thinking of her when he said in a lecture at St. Benedict Center: "Every one of us was rich enough to have had a girl give us freely substance and blood and life and breath! The nine months' assignment of a dear girl's travail and pain and love has brought each one of us into the world! We were purchased by a great price—not in a group, but singularly. And our mothers looked on us for a long time as if we were the only one in existence. There was only one baby to our mothers while we were in the cradle, only one coo!"

Of the four children in the family of three boys and one girl, he was undoubtedly his mother's favorite. There never was even the slightest misunderstanding between them. Mrs. Feeney appreciated her son's genius, and took pride in it, but neither annoyed him by preaching nor embarrassed him by praising or pushing him before others. She allowed him to develop on his own. He was never suffocated by her love, for she was the embodiment of tact and possessed that supreme feminine wisdom which tells a woman when to leave a man alone. On the other hand, she was always there when he needed her.

His relations with his father were more complicated. Like many great men and their great or greater sons, they were more rivals than friends. He used to tell with enormous relish how his mother was always on his side when he fought with his father, though she never said a word. He sensed her support and she sensed his guilelessness. She also knew the Irish propensity for fighting and forgetting. Only once did she interfere—when she was afraid the fight had gone too far. She took her talented son aside and said quietly, "I know papa is difficult, dear. But don't forget, if I had married a man of my own intelligence, instead of being the brilliant boy I'm so proud of, you'd be a little boob sitting on the front lawn." From his father, he inherited his elan, his intense personality, his vitality of speaking, and his brilliance of mind, as Mrs. Feeney so graciously conceded.

II

Leonard Feeney's small-town world changed when he entered the Jesuit order at seventeen. If he was unhappy during his fourteen years of formation until ordination, he didn't reveal it to anyone at the time. He was sick a lot, perhaps because of the strain of his phenomenal academic achievement. He was in and out of hospitals, and from one of them he glumly appraised his health to a brother: "I am still pretty incapacitated, I give myself about 49 or 50%." This was his usual physical condition.

He was sent for graduate work to Oxford University where one of his professors, Lord David Cecil, reported, "I am getting more from my association with Leonard Feeney than he could possibly get from me." The student was in his twenties when Lord Cecil paid his high tribute, very unusual coming from an Oxford don. But no one who knew Leonard Feeney considered it unusual.

It is difficult to think of Leonard Feeney as a novice and actually he was an individualistic one. He disliked regimentation and in those pre-Vatican II days there was plenty of it in the religious orders. Self-confidence, initiative, and originality were not encouraged. Underdogs were made to feel they were just that—underdogs. However, Leonard Feeney was rarely faulted in chapter—"because you've been sick and we know you could not take it," intoned one superior, starchily. Leonard Feeney also skirted nineteenth century spirituality with its emphasis on external performance, pompous protocol, and puritan morals. There was plenty of that around, too, and he avoided it all. It wasn't fashionable to do so in those days. Yet he was very docile and so escaped discipline and graduated *summa cum laude* at the end of his seminary training.

In his early thirties he started attracting attention in the Catholic literary world by his poetry, essays, short stories, sketches, and dramatizations written with humor and verse. By 1934, Catholics in America began to realize he was a priest who had style, who had wit, who had words, and something to say with them. He was in demand for lectures at their colleges, and talks at their communion breakfasts in places like the Waldorf Astoria, and eventually was put on the radio Sunday nights. It was their hour, the "Catholic Hour." He complained that on Sunday nights a radio speaker had stiff competition from "contraltos, commentators, and comedians—none of which I am." He needn't have worried. He held his audience spellbound from the beginning. His magnetic voice and dominant personality seemed to reach each one, singularly.

In his first talk he said, "You came from nowhere, brought here by God's omnipotence, especially chosen for existence because He loved you, and now that you are, you will ever be. God does not expect you to be different than He made you, either. All He asks in return for the greater gift of creation is that you be yourself. 'Will you be John Jones or Mary Smith for Me?' God asks each one of us, 'Will you be big or small, young or old, good-looking or not, with many talents or few, just as I planned you? If you will, and will bear the burden of being yourself for a few years on this earth for Me, then I shall be your God for all eternity. I shall be your Father, your Friend, your Protector. I shall always interpret you with sympathy and understanding. Others may think they know how wicked you are for they see in your sins what has been consented to; but I shall always remember what has been resisted, and the struggles you have made to keep at least something in you fine and innocent and pure. I shall be your Defender against your enemies, and no one will dare to speak unkindly of you without having to settle a score with Me. I shall be the faithful Watcher at your bedside when you are ill, or tired, or uninteresting. For you will never be uninteresting to Me, never a bother, never a bore. You will always be my creature, infinitely fascinating, whom I made out of nothing for my own celestial purposes. You will always be my loved one, always my child.' "

The audience, mostly Catholic, loved this kind of dignified utterance and sincerity—rare on the air. They felt a sense of rapport and intimacy when Father Feeney stepped in front of the microphone. The more intelligent of his listeners found him intellectually exciting while the less gifted were flattered and proud that for once a Catholic priest was giving them their money's worth.

His energy, his anxious, intense personality, his vigorous mind and character attracted those who loved the Faith as well as those who hated it. He spoke dramatically and that was part of his nature. He admitted of himself, "I overstate things. My friends have rebuked me for it. I have tried to correct it. But I haven't. I can't. I say 'most' when I mean 'much'. Without the words 'tremendous', 'wonderful', 'amazing', and 'astounding', my vocabulary would collapse. I couldn't talk. I couldn't think!"

He loved the dogmas of the Church and had a unique talent for inspiring others to love them. In one of his articles he explained the difficult doctrine of the Blessed Trinity with such lucidity and drama as well as precision that for years it was required reading in many seminaries. Then when he was silenced, the Seminary Elders saw to it that the article was shelved. It began by stating simply: "The Blessed Trinity is not a puzzle. It is not a trick. It is an innocent, profound statement of how life exists in Him Who *is* Life. A mystery is not a fact about which we can know nothing. It is a fact about which we cannot know everything. But the deeper we plunge, the more we learn."[2]

Frank Sheed, a long-time friend and one of his publishers, said, "For Father Feeney, dogma is not only true; it is breathlessly exciting. That is his special vocation...to make his readers feel the thrill." One reason for Father Feeney's success was his instinct for putting first things first. He believed that the Church should not be explained or even discussed in terms of its non-essentials like "incense, holy water, relics, and such incidentals."[3] He concentrated on the Trinity, the Eucharist, the

[2]*The Leonard Feeney Omnibus*, "Outlines," pp. 183-184.
[3]*Omnibus*, "Fish on Friday," p. 3.

Incarnation, the Sacraments, and the Virgin Mother. He was extremely incarnational and so integrated nature and grace that he never spoke of one without including the other.

He could talk long and well on anything, and his style was quite his own. Like G. K. Chesterton whom he called "a tank of paradoxygen" few could beat him at impromptu versifying, punning, and paradox. He met Arthur Guiterman and within minutes had improvised:

> Here's to Arthur Guiterman,
> The famous rime and meter man.
> For making verse
> That's trim and terse
> I never met a neater man.

Naturally his reputation soared. He was like a pied piper, never without a crowd of friends flocking after him to enjoy his performance. The simplest situations became dramatic under the magic fire of his mind, and his legend grew. His wit was natural, spontaneous, and lavish. He was introduced to a Mr. Case and quipped, "I hope your first name is Justin." He accosted a florist named John D. Lyons and said the John should be changed to Dan. He preferred a long-established oil company to a new one, he said, "because there's no fuel like an old fuel." He thought he ought to bow his head whenever he used the word "exegesis" lest he be accused of profanity. He heard that a hen had won a prize for hatching almost 200 eggs in one year, and remarked that the hen deserved the Pulletser prize. Unaware that he had a personality essentially individual, he wrote: "If one is a Catholic, one cannot think without being cosmical or without being comical either, because the Faith links all realities together and fills the world with surprises."

By 1940 he was moving freely and frequently in the highest circles of New York with well-known figures like Sinclair Lewis, Dorothy Thompson, Jacques Maritain, T. S. Eliot, Noel Coward, Fulton J. Sheen, and others. But he preferred people like taxi-cab drivers, dock-workers, janitors, and waiters. They were the simple of heart and he called them "the soundest of all metaphysicians and under the influence of divine grace, the profoundest of all mystics." He saw beneath their unpretentious exterior honesty, loyalty, directness, and dogged devotion to a priest like him. He was never patronizing or condescending to these uneducated people. He accepted them as they were and they accepted him. He won their respect and their love to the end. Perhaps he sensed that the adulation of the rich is apt to be as empty as their riches. Certainly his time of popularity was running out. It was 1942 and the hand-writing was already on the wall. The day he walked into St. Benedict Center was the beginning of the end.

III

St. Benedict Center started modestly. Its purpose was to bolster the faith of Catholic students at Harvard and neighboring colleges by supplying them with Catholic books and also, as its founder, Catherine Clarke, pointed out, "to establish a place where non-Catholics could find out from Catholics what the Church was teaching."

At first there was no priest. But as the students and their questions multiplied, Catherine Clarke, a woman of charming personality and great magnetism, appealed to the Jesuits for Leonard Feeney. At the time, 1942, he was at the height of his literary and lecturing career. Nevertheless he was appointed to the Center and from then on *that*, and not his writing or lecturing, became his simple, full-time dedication. The thirty-six years of life remaining to him were devoted exclusively to St. Benedict Center whose apostolate was, in the words of its founder, "the preservation and propagation of the doctrines of the Church." With incredible enthusiasm and tremendous energy Father Feeney worked at St. Benedict Center as if no other place and no other apostolate existed.

In Leonard Feeney's hand, the Center soon became a lively place of theological study and zeal for the Catholic Faith. With Catherine Clarke's presence, it kept its familial, warm, and friendly atmosphere. The combination attracted hundreds of students, professors, priests, prelates, and notables from Father's previous literary career. "As soon as you walked into the Center," wrote one of his admirers, "you would be aware of Father. A compact, dark-eyed, endlessly mobile figure, loosely contained in a Jesuit cassock (I look like a character in a Saroyan play, was his description of himself), he seemed the very proto-type of the 'dynamic personality'. You might find him at the blackboard, furiously covering it with diagrams and symbols to facilitate an instruction on the meaning of person and nature in the hypostatic union; or slumped down in his huge red leather chair, reading aloud and expounding on the poetry of Gerard Manley Hopkins; or entertaining a newcomer with one of his convulsively-funny impersonations (the trick was to put a likely subject on an unlikely topic—FDR on the state of the Church; Al Smith on Descartes; Fulton Sheen on Coca-Cola)."[4]

Father Feeney was not an administrator nor an efficiency expert. He was not an organizer. But he was quintessentially a priest and father. This "priestliness" of his was so strongly projected that no matter how many priests came to St. Benedict Center, or were quoted or talked about or referred to, Leonard Feeney was the only one called simply, "Father."

Oblivious to politics, wealth, appearances, and with little understanding or interest in the things of this world, he con-centrated on what a priest should be for his children and declared, "No matter how pitiable or regrettable is the condition of our children, we never abandon them, never disown them, or feel that there is any emergency of their lives to which we are not

[4]*The Center Review*, Spring 1978.

equal with a Father's compassion, a Father's reverence, and a Father's love."[5] With this outlook which he lived to the fullest, he won the devotion and the love of youthful, middle-aged, and elderly enthusiastic, idealistic followers.

He gave them what they wanted a priest to give them, what they knew a priest by profession should give them—answers to the relentless questions men ask themselves in the inmost region of their souls: What is the purpose of life? Where am I going? Why is there suffering?

Father Feeney was at his best with the Greek New Testament in his hands. He felt that Holy Scripture was full of inexhaustible treasures for those who were simple and innocent of heart. Combining evangelical ardor with catholic charm, he insisted on the primacy of the Gospels; and soon the bookstores around Harvard Square started running out of Bibles. With resourcefulness and originality he explained the Gospel narratives, pacing up and down, and translating them as he went along. "St. Mary Magdalen adored Our Lord's divinity by kissing His feet. What greater tribute could you pay to God than to give Him all of your being: your kisses, your tears, and your hair?— the solid, the liquid, and the hairy states of your being." Or commenting on the story of the Gerasenes, and gesticulating rapidly, "When a Man can come into a town and, without apologizing, send 1,000 pigs into the sea and have the townspeople beg Him to leave, and He doesn't have to give a weak, cowardly explanation, I know that I have Authority on my hands."

After twenty-five years of separation from him, Avery Dulles wrote, "There are certain texts from the Bible that I can never read without hearing, in my imagination, the voice and intonation of Leonard Feeney. Among them is the following: 'I have fought the good fight, I have finished the race, I have kept the faith.' These words should serve as Leonard Feeney's epitaph. They express his overriding concern to resist any dilution of the Christian Faith and to pass it on entire, as a precious heritage, to the generations yet to come."[6]

His ability to establish intimacy between himself and his listeners was uncanny. "Never have I known a speaker with such a sense of collective psychology," writes Avery Dulles. "Totally aware of the reactions of every person in the room, he would focus his attention especially on those who seemed hostile, indifferent, or distracted. When at length he had the entire audience reacting as a unit, he would launch into the main body of his talk, leading them from insight to insight, from emotion to emotion, until all were carried away, as if by an invisible force permeating the atmosphere."[7]

He spoke personally and convincingly: "You don't belong to yourself; you haven't signatured the world with too much ownership; there is Somebody higher and bigger who planned your bones; there is something in you never arranged by yourself, called conscience, telling you when something is wrong. Even apart from Revelation you can become aware of the existence of a personal, intelligent God just by a study of the world. It would be cruel if God had designed a world and left no reflection of Himself in it, as if He were some sort of Cubist. The world has His signature there for us to see and to make us aware that there is a God behind it."

Incapable of being a party man or politician, he was never afraid to hit hard at error in high places. Summoned by a student at Harvard to administer to a suicide attempt, he turned on the dean who quietly murmured, "Dreadfully unfortunate!" and

[6]*America*, February 25, 1978, p. 137.
[7]*Ibid.*, p. 135.

demanded, "What do you expect him to do when you teach him he's a bunch of electrons descended from a monkey?" For Leonard Feeney to witness an intellectual's politeness in the face of tragedy was like waving a red flag before a bull. He considered such studied politeness an utter sham. "Its credentials in academic circles (which vouch for its kindred behavior everywhere) are," he wrote, "the subdued voice, the indefinite reference, the qualified statement, the sustained smile."[8]

He was especially hard on pseudo-intellectuals and enjoyed reviling them in verse:

> I know their game: each self-exhorted
> and solipsistically sorted,
> Fancies his own support supported.

Father Feeney spoke spontaneously and with authority. He expected to be listened to, and he was, for his arguments were ontologically sound. He impressed his hearers by his logic even when they disagreed with his conclusions.

"God can create," he said vigorously in one of his lectures. "He can also annihilate. Of course He does not annihilate by acting, but by ceasing to act where He had been acting before."

"If you are childlike of heart," he used to say, "you know two things about the world: that it isn't God, and that it couldn't be without a God. But it takes humility to know God. Pride likes to destroy Him. An atheist is a proud, academic snob who snubs all the minds of history who have seen order where he says there is none. He loves to be infinite enough to destroy Infinity."

Father Feeney continued to pack them in as his kudos grew. Certain positive characteristics were noted whenever he spoke: his devotion to the Blessed Sacrament, his love for the Blessed

---

[8]"Catholicism is Also a Manner."

Mother, his admiration of nuns and his respect for women. Two great women had influenced his own life: Delia Leonard Feeney, his mother, and Catherine Goddard Clarke, the foundress of St. Benedict Center.

Professors and students poured in to hear what he had to say. If they looked for drama, they weren't disappointed. Every story he told was unforgettable perhaps because invariably it inculcated a deep principle which remained to help someone in a moment of need long after the mere enjoyment of the story had passed. One of his favorite stories concerned a Jesuit bishop who had taken a vow of perfection. The Jesuits invited him to dinner and watched him like ferrets to see what he would do. He did nothing more than surprise them by asking for wine, win them by his simplicity, and delight them by cracking jokes. Father Feeney commented, "When piety is genuine, it is always attractive. If it isn't fascinating, it isn't the Faith."

Father Feeney sharply resented Catholics who were on the defensive with touchy subjects like the Inquisition. "Jews used to beg to be tried by the Inquisition, it was so fair," he'd snap, vigorously rubbing his hands together. Instead of apologizing for the sale of indulgences or explaining that the Popes had never said you could buy your way into heaven with one, he scowled and said, "I wish there were someone in our world today with enough faith to buy one!" This was often his way of waking up a lethargic faith. He called it his own "shock treatment."

The encomiums mounted, the crowds increased, but so did the criticism. He was compared to Athanasius *contra mundum*, Jerome, and Joan of Arc, Ximenes, Erasmus, and Leon Bloy. As the comparisons became more pejorative, the buzz got louder. More and more he became known for teaching fearlessly the unpopular doctrine that outside the Church there is no salvation. He and his disciples found plenty of direct quotes from the earliest Church Fathers to notables of modern times, from Cyprian and Origen, and medieval popes and saints, to Orestes

Brownson and Cardinal Newman.[9] "The overzealous members of St. Benedict Center had the best of it on the basis of centuries-old dogma and Church practice," wrote one prominent theologian.

Many of his listeners converted to Catholicism. This caused trouble. It was just the tip of the iceberg. Some entered religious life because of his direction. This caused even more trouble. More ice. But the real trouble began with a few enthusiasts who, unendowed with his genius and genuineness, imitated or misinterpreted his personal peculiarities of style. They lacked imagination and they didn't have his charismatic appeal. They didn't distinguish dogmas from dialectics nor essentials from externals. Their apocalypses and exaggerations bred a reaction which led to severe ecclesiastical censures. Idealistic, impractical, and too integral to be disloyal to his supporters, Father Feeney jumped after them into the troubled waters which soon were closing in over their heads. The entire Center was placed under interdict and Father Feeney was silenced.

Those who knew when to leave left the Center fast. Of the hundreds who had partaken of its hospitality for years, only a handful remained indomitable. Father Feeney was proud of those who stayed with him during his censured years. He kept their spirits up by reminding them of the Crusade they were fighting. "Everyone knows what you are, my dear children. Everyone knows you are not a little local gang but that you are from all over the world, every environment, and every antecedent. Everybody knows what you are standing for. It is clear and sheer."

"We don't have many crowds," he declared sadly a few weeks after his silencing, "but it gives us an opportunity to gather our

[9] See Thomas R. Ryan, C.PP.S., *Orestes Brownson, A Definitive Biography*, p. 286.

forces and learn the things we ought to know. Nothing helps us
more than our siege. Now we can sit down and prepare. We are
very well prepared now but we'll be even better prepared if they
keep away for six or seven months more." His infectious opti-
mism was shared by his followers, most of whom were young.
But, suddenly falling back on the prophetic insight he displayed
so often during his life, he inserted a note which had disquieting
overtones. "Of course," he paused and his well-modulated voice
caught the attention of his youthful audience who listened in
stunned silence as he added, "if they come next week, we'll let
them in; but, if they don't . . ." Then he broke off, stared calmly
into space as if into the future for a few seconds, turned abruptly
on his heel and strode from the room.

Twenty-five years were to pass before the censures were lifted
and the crowds returned.

IV

After his silencing in 1949, Leonard Feeney was a man beset
by criticism and hostility. At times it appeared his nerves were at
the breaking point as one approbrium after another came his
way.

However, for a man of his temperament, drama perhaps was
necessary. Perhaps life had to be one crisis after another. At any
rate, if Father Feeney needed an arena his followers happily saw
to it he had one. Fiercely devoted to him and he to them, they
formed themselves into a religious congregation with private
vows. Many had been fired from their jobs, disowned or dis-
inherited by their families, and ostracized by their friends. They
banned together and vowed to make the first consideration of
their lives the doctrinal crusade of St. Benedict Center with
Father Feeney as their leader. Now all their problems were completely his, spiritual as well as mundane.

Father Feeney was as unfitted for practical affairs as he was
fitted for idealistic. His mission was to inspire rather than to do.

He used to say jokingly that God alone chose him to lead a religious community, that he was no good as a superior, that the Jesuits knew this and consequently wouldn't have had him as a headwaiter. (His followers agreed with God).

Fortunately Catherine Goddard Clarke was the co-foundress, and in her capable, astutely practical hands, the Center kept afloat. Father Feeney was glad to leave food, finances, and practical details to her while he continued to inspire.

A constant phrase of his was: "Never a dull moment." There never was with him around. Every now and then visitors would come. The results were unpredictable. He usually dismissed them after a hard-hitting lecture on the importance of doctrine. Father Feeney's gift for versifying came in handy. On one memorable occasion, after trouncing a well-known visitor he composed:

> I must regret my partings more,
> Renounce, not just refuse,
> And make a face, and pace the floor,
> And burst into boo-hoos,
> When someone ambles out the door,
> I am so pleased to lose.

His childlike frankness could be very amusing, annoying, or embarrassing, depending on the recipient. The more pompous the person, the more amusing his exiting would be, of course. Undoubtedly many people didn't come because they were scared off by the interdict. But there were others even more scared of Father Feeney.

In 1958, Father Feeney and his community moved from Cambridge, Massachusetts and Harvard Square to a farm in Harvard, Massachusetts. There they were able to follow a monastic life of prayer, study, and manual labor which had for years fascinated Father Feeney.

He continued to attack pseudo-intellectuals. "God didn't make the world for intellectual outlooks. Take the sky. It isn't intellectually arranged. If it were, the big stars would be in one place and the little stars in another and not the disordered order there is. Intellectualism wants everything schemed and mathematized and made into formulas."

And a slap shot at seminary training...

Imagine what a situation it is for the Church when moral theology has gone haywire to such an extent that the Holy Father had to warn the priests recently that they are not allowed to tell what they hear in confession to psychiatrists!

And the Universities...

At Harvard and M.I.T. they have all the equipment and test tubes in the world, but I defy them to make one, tiny little seed to put into the ground. They can tell you how much nitrogen and sulfur is in a seed, but I defy them to make one. They hope to come to that someday: they think that the discovery of the manufacture of life is just around the corner. And they would a billion times rather discover a tiny molecule of life than adore and love the life God had already made. They would one thousand times rather take an entity, like a lily or a rose, and tear it to pieces to see how it is constructed in the hopes of giving God competition than leave it in its beauty and give God contemplation and love.

On the positive side, Father Feeney kept his followers excited by his original insights and lucidity of thought. He taught them how to pray: "In order to put ourselves in prayers, we must first put ourselves into the presence of God. There is a way of doing that spiritually, and it is to realize that God's time is always 'now'. God's time is always now; but our time is never now; our instant is always fleeting."

His advice was encouraging and trenchant: "Never mind what you did yesterday—whether it be good or bad! And, don't mind what you are going to do tomorrow! Don't even mind what you are going to do an hour from now! Let that go!"

He led his followers gently: "God is more delighted with our efforts than with our results, because God loves us as children. Did you ever see a child learning to speak? It is not his results that delight you, it is his effort. Sometimes you are more fascinated with a word that comes close to the word, than the word fully and completely enunciated. That is the delight of effort. Thanks be to God, it is the same with our struggle towards eternity."

He warned them against complicated methods: "Don't be anxious to be too recollected all of a sudden. I don't mind recollection at the conclusion of your efforts, but I hate it as the process by which you achieve it. Most people—as soon as they find out you are looking for recollection—give you so many things in advice, that it is more distracting than distraction. You start distractedly studying your own recollections. So, take one little thing at a time."

He was personal in his advice and that was effective: "I said once to God, and I think He might have liked this, 'I am greatly distracted in Your presence; but I would rather be distracted in Your presence, than recollected in anybody else's.' "

Slowly his apostolate on the outside grew. The years had mellowed everyone and the bitterness began to be forgotten.

Father Feeney's original mind and sincere manner won a host of new friends, many of them non-Catholic. "You know, dear, I'm going to pray that you become a Catholic. Isn't that mean?" he'd disclose to elderly Yankee men and women, several of whom he succeeded in converting. Often they were surprised that more Catholics weren't standing by him. As Frank Sheed wrote, "When Boniface VIII said in the bull *Unam Sanctam* that it was 'altogether necessary for salvation for every human creature to be subject to the Roman Pontiff', he seemed to be saying not only what Father Feeney was condemned for saying, but what a vast number of yesterday's Catholics had grown up believing."[10] A vast number of yesterday's Protestants thought so, too, and they respected Father Feeney and were not antagonized by his stand.

No one was ever with him for long without being told of Jesus and Mary. At home or away, his first interest was, "Are you a Catholic?" and his second, "Do you go to Mass and Communion regularly?" if you were; or, "Wouldn't you like to become a child of Mary?" if you weren't—or "Won't you at least say a Hail Mary with me?" if you didn't seem receptive. Here was the true greatness of Father Feeney: he knew that only God was worth having and would go to great lengths to get Him to everyone.

That is why his direct approach rarely repelled people. They sensed his sincerity and were pleased by his genuine interest in their souls. They knew, too, he was different. "He was like no other priest ever encountered," wrote one of his disciples, "an irrepressible and irresistible field of force."

In 1972, through the dedicated efforts of Bishop Flanagan of Worcester, Cardinal Medeiros of Boston, Cardinal Wright of the Sacred Congregation of the Clergy, and the good offices of the Trappist Abbey of Spencer, Massachusetts, the ecclesiastical censures against Father Feeney were lifted. He was 75 years old.

At this point, it would be nice to have a storybook ending, describing the peaceful old age and happy death of Father Leonard Feeney, surrounded by loving disciples. Alas, it was the very contrary. In the five years of life remaining to him, Father Leonard Feeney was to hit the very depths of grief. His order, to which he was deeply committed, split into two, three, and eventually four divisions. Catherine Clarke was no longer around to help him pick up the pieces. She had died four years earlier of Hodgkin's disease.

[10]*The Church and I*, p. 166.

Berated and blamed by certain members for not taking sides, the elderly priest would often break down like a child and weep. Incredibly this only engendered hostility. A victim of Parkinson's disease, his health steadily declining, he continued to be pulled apart, caught between all groups. He loved every one of his followers and he tried to unite them, but his efforts came to naught. Groping pathetically for answers he couldn't find, the old man would give up and sit helplessly by the hour, staring in a solitary, silent grief.

A lonely genius, set apart from others, supersensitive, unprotected, and helpless, he died on January 30, 1978. The painful hours of his last week on earth bring to mind what he had written years before: "All alone, God died in the supremest martyrdom that ever could be. We who die are privileged to die with Jesus. If we die apart from Him, it is routine death, which even the undertaker will soon forget. If we die for the sake of Him, it is a martyrdom which even the angels will remember."[11]

The *Catholic Free Press* of Worcester, Massachusetts, in a moving obituary editorial stated:

> ...Father Feeney...because of the clarity of his thought, won for himself a lasting place in the history of the Church in America.... What he said, what he was, what he did, was part of the history of his times.

One of Father Feeney's spiritual sons developed that theme: "Whether history's final assessment of Father will be accurate and just we cannot be sure," he writes, "history being as liable to fallibility as any other human process. Certainly Father was too great and complex a figure to slip neatly into any historian's easy categories. It is almost inevitable that the portrait that will eventually emerge will be of a diminished figure; the magic will be

[11]*Bread of Life*, p. 199.

missing, so that what is gained by way of perspective will be lost by way of dimension. Still, one thing at least seems certain. Whatever else may be said of him, the name of Leonard Feeney will henceforth be inseparably linked with the notion that Christ and His Church are the central, single, enduring hope of the world. And, in the end, that is probably all he would want."[12]

*   *   *

Father Feeney lies buried at St. Benedict Center beneath the silent ground of Still River, the little town which witnessed his greatest joys, his deepest griefs, and the triumph and desolation of his closing years.

S. M. CLARE

[12]*The Center Review,* Spring 1978.

Leonard Feeney and his parents

Leonard Feeney in the Jesuit novitiate, New York

Leonard Feeney, front center, as a Jesuit novic

Leonard Feeney as a young priest

Leonard Feeney age 38

Catherine Goddard Clarke and Leonard Feeney

Leonard Feeney at St. Benedict Center,
Cambridge, Massachusetts

Survival Till Seventeen

Survival Till Seventeen
SOME PORTRAITS OF EARLY IDEAS

———◆———

THE VOICE

DURING the first year of my life, I lay in the cradle and mumbled innumerable sounds into which it was impossible to read any meanings.

At the age of one, I began experimenting with the syllables of the English language, and six months later spoke my first sentence. My parents were startled to discover that one of the words contained in it was "Damn!"—an expletive picked up—so my parents hasten to assure me—from a tramp who came begging at our door and was invited in for coffee.

Although such a precocious display of profanity might well have induced my parents to believe that I was destined to become a desperado, they had the unique consolation of remembering that I had been born into this world free from the guilt of original sin. This extraordinary privilege came as a result of my having been baptized some hours before birth at a moment when it seemed certain that the price of my life was to have been my mother's death.

Among the very few papers in my possession which might be honored with the dignity of being called "notes" is the certificate of my birth, a copy of which I secured some years ago from the Registry of Births in my native city. It is such a decisive, laconic, frightening document, that I have often stared at it with something of the feeling one might have if he could tip-toe into his own nursery and find himself asleep in his own crib. The document remarks, concerning an existence which is indubitably mine:

NAME OF CHILD: Leonard Edward Feeney
DATE OF BIRTH: Feb. 15, 1897
SEX: Male
COLOR: White
PLACE OF BIRTH: 118 Adams Street, Lynn, Mass.
FATHER'S NAME: Thomas Butler Feeney
MOTHER'S MAIDEN NAME: Delia Agnes Leonard

It was the original intention of my parents to give me no middle name, but by a combination of my father's and my mother's family names, to make my own a happy union of the two. The Edward was thrown in at Baptism in honor of my Uncle Edward, who was my sponsor, but was thrown out later after we had satisfied him with this courtesy.

When I went to school I came to believe that Leonard derived from the Latin words: *leonis ardor*, meaning "fierceness of a lion," and I was wont to boast of this signification. Some years later, however, I met an Italian priest in Florence named Leonardo, and he told me that our name is taken straightforwardly from the Latin: *leo* and *nardus*, meaning "lion and spikenard," and rendered freely as "strength and fragrance" or "strength and healing." However gracefully he put it, I was not pleased with the new translation. I preferred being "a wild lion" to being a "sweet lion," and wish I had been left under my original illusion.

This same queer feeling of an identity retroactively experienced by looking at a birth certificate, was also mine a few years ago when I was examining an old family album, and came upon a picture of a small boy named Leonard, snapped at the age of ten, on his front lawn, by way of exhibiting how dressed-up he looked in a new Easter suit and hat. I felt impelled at the time to commemorate my emotion (one of the

oddest human experience has to offer) by pencilling a few
lines under the picture which ran as follows:

> So that's me, taken on the lawn,
> At ten,
> In my new Sunday hat!
> Good Lord, have I been going on,
> Since then,
> And was I that?

But let us go back again to my infancy for a few more
hurried observations.

My mother was eighteen when she married, and I am her
oldest child. She is now in her sixties, and by way of describing her—if now, *a fortiori* then—I can only repeat what an
astute observer said of her in my hearing not long ago: "She
is like a little doll!"

My mother claims that my father was her first and only
beau, and I believe her. My father disavows this, maintaining
with great emphasis that when he married my mother, she
had in her keeping a letter written her by another suitor and
inscribed to her "in his own blood." My mother says it was not
"in his own blood" but "in red ink." My father insists it was
not "in red ink" but "in his own blood." And thus they argue
back and forth, and have been doing so since I first met them.
My father seems inordinately proud of the fact that he was
able to wrest the hand of my mother from the clutches of such
a gory rival. My mother, on the other hand, grows indignant
at the accusation of having been associated in any way with
such a Bluebeard. At all events, whatever pigment stained the
precious paper, it has since been either destroyed or lost
("destroyed" says my father, "lost" says my mother), and so
historians will be left forever in the dark concerning this
sanguinary phase of my parental past.

One romantic experience of my mother's before marriage,
she herself will admit. One would need to know first hand

my mother's radiant innocence—an innocence uniquely possessed by immigrant girls who are at once Catholic and Irish —to appreciate both the charm of the following story, and the guilelessness which induces my mother to tell it.

"One day," says my mother, "when I was seventeen, I was riding in the train from Boston to Lynn. A young man came in and sat beside me. He was quite handsome, and handsomely dressed. He had the most elegant manners. He was a travelling salesman. We talked all the way from Boston to Lynn. When we were about to leave the train, he invited me to take dinner with him at one of the hotels. I was tempted to accept the invitation, because he was the soul of courtesy. But something inside me grew frightened, and something my mother once told me as a child kept saying 'Don't!' So I said 'No!' and I didn't." . . . Then there is a pause, and my mother looks at you sharply with her challenging grey eyes and says, half reflectively, half in interrogation, "Wasn't I the coward?"

This is my mother, pro and con.

Genealogy is a fascinating pursuit, and I have often wanted to investigate mine for the sake of studying certain unexplainable traits in my nature. On my mother's side our roots are easily retraceable. We are, through her, of the O'Briens of County Clare, Irish pure and undefiled, possessed of the quiet gentleness of the West Coast folk, and with as reasonable a claim as any to have descended from Brian Boru, County Clare's great warrior and king. On my father's side our ancestry is more difficult to review.

My father, who is often mistaken for an Italian, is a mixture of Irish ingrained with Spanish. This latter strain would account for his swarthy complexion and terribly dark eyes, eyes that scrutinize you as though you dwelt in a dungeon. He has been fairly copied in looks by each of his four children, since none of us resembles my mother. But it has often struck me that there is little of the authentic Latin in my father's temperament, or in ours. We possess the Latin excitability, but not the Latin repose. We gesticulate precisely and close to the body, never in the expansive full-flung fashion of Southern Europe. We are sensitive without being quarrelsome, and our impetuosity, which is unpredictable, is interspersed with sudden bursts of caution. It is one of the strongest hunches of my life that what passes in us for Spanish blood is really something too fantastic to mention. Our modal quality of thought is different from all our kindred, and our Celtic lightheartedness is chastened, and sometimes completely shut off, by bursts of mysterious and exotic loneliness, occasionally verging on despair.

A mathematician standing in the Garden of Eden when Adam and Eve were being banished, and endeavoring at the time to quote the odds against our chances for existence, would be driven into a problem in differential calculus containing so many numerical symbols and such a vast procession of zeros, that all the forests of the world would scarcely supply him with paper sufficient on which to make the estimate. He would give us up as a bad job and say that it was mathematically certain that none of us should ever be.

And yet, we are! We are by reason of a million romances that came out correctly. In each generation there were the necessary infants who invariably survived the wars, the plagues, the famines and the pestilences of history, matured to the age of courtship, were mellowed with the enticements of love, and became the acceptable bridegrooms and consenting brides requisite for prolonging the pattern of the human race to the point where we took on. Some years ago I attempted to express this profundity in a verse, which ran as follows:

> When I said Mass at Christmas
> And candles were aglow,
> I saw a white old woman,
> Two thousand years ago:

My very great grandmother,
Who spun me flesh and bone,
Who felt my fingers aching
In the atoms of her own,

In whom my eyes were shining,
However far away,
When Christ was in His cradle
And it was Christmas Day!

This verse, executed, as I supposed, in a moment of high seriousness, was accepted by most of my critics as a piece of whimsy; for I have suffered under the curse of being considered a whimsical poet, and have been laughed at when I thought to make others cry.

Be that as it may, it is with extreme seriousness that I contemplate a certain summer evening years ago, in a little cottage by the sea, overlooking the rocks on the North Shore of Massachusetts, just at the point where King's Beach in Lynn is separated from Fisherman's Beach in Swampscott, where my mother in a light blue dress and a summer hat disporting a streamer, was invited to "spend the evening" with some friends. By a lightning-like stroke of *timing* on the part of the Providence of God, it happened that my father was there too, airing his Irish idiom, flashing his Spanish eyes. It need not be said that my existence hung by a thread on every item of that meeting: on the fact that my mother chose to be there instead of elsewhere; on the fact that the conveyance brought her early and not late; on the detail of her seeming more attractively dressed for the summer evening than any of the other young ladies. My existence likewise depended on the avoidance of anything that might have kept my father away, such as a rash from poison ivy, or the throbbing of a sore tooth.

It was a pleasant gathering, so I am told, and everybody enjoyed everybody else's company, particularly my father my mother's. There was the gaiety and song appropriate to a group of merry exiles dwelling in a Puritan stronghold by the beaches of the North Shore. There was ginger ale for the girls, which makes them giggle, and beer for the young men, which makes them bothersome. My mother in her light blue dress and delicate manners easily prevailed, and my father was taken captive by the little steamer dangling from her hat.

There was a short courtship, a sudden proposal, and a very simple marriage. Everything happened precisely at the right time, just as it had been accurately happening all through the ages A. D. and B. C., back through the eras of the dripping hourglass, back through the clockless centuries of the caveman, back to the early pages of Genesis and the first meeting of a maid and a man. Even my conception occurred exactly at the time when God had planned it. The child arriving in our home at any other season or year which was not the winter of 1897 would have been my brother or my sister, not myself. And what chronicle he or she would care to write concerning the same parents, or what tribute pay them for an existence not mine, must be left in the realm of the sheerly metaphysical.

I am not a child psychologist, nor indeed a psychologist of any kind, but I should like to offer some of the experiences of my early childhood for clinical examination by those capable of appraising such things scientifically.

It is my belief that in those years of a child's life which antecede the use of reason, when his mind is slumbering in a world of sensations and playthings, there are definite moments when the intellect leaps forward, so to speak, ahead of its cue, takes in some situation by swift intuition or insight, makes a judgment—and then returns to dawdle on in its haze of simple apprehensions. I can recall three such experiences happening to me before the age of six.

The first occurred when I was four, and was brought into the parlor to see my grandmother lying in her coffin. Frankly, I did not know I had a grandmother at all until I found her dead. Then, for one brief instant of reasoned consciousness, which I can recapture now as vividly as when it first occurred, I looked at the lifeless form of my grandmother and said to myself, if not in the maturity of these words, at least with the absolute clarity of this idea: "Oh! So there is death attached to this business of life! And this is the way we all end!" . . . An hour later, my grandmother, living or dead, had infinitely less interest for me than a shadow dancing on the wall of my playroom, or a rubber ball rolling elusively across the floor.

My second experience with the use of reason in an embryo stage (my mother declares I was five at the time) was when I heard a woman say to my mother concerning another woman who was suffering from asthma, that she was *drinking kerosene oil for a cure!* Upon hearing this, I paused long enough to wrinkle my brow and soliloquize: "This is a queer world I have gotten into!"; and then went back to the logger-headedness of my normal development, paying no further attention to what my mother and the other woman had to say to each other.

The last incident of this kind, in which I executed a premature judgment with a definite awareness of mind, occurred, according to my best calculations, in the summer of the year in which I was six years old, and brings back to me my mother's voice calling through the kitchen window . . . calling across the fields, over the hedges, through the trees . . . calling desperately to whatever place I was lost in and could not be found . . . calling in the poignancy of a beautiful tone over-pitched in its anxiety . . . calling with the uncertain tremor that is attached to the airing of one's private shame to the other open windows of the neighborhood, behind which halting housewives listen suspiciously and are anxious, in their jungle maternity, to gather little trickles of evidence that will establish flaws in their neighbors' children and magnify virtues in their own . . . calling once, twice, a half a dozen times, into the indefinite spaces of the hot noon hours . . . calling plaintively with a combined crescendo of fatigue and alarm which the light vocal powers of a slender girl are not strong enough to support in an appropriate key:

"Len . . . errrrrrd! If you don't come in now for dinner, you won't get any pudding!"

The voice—or its echo—at last reached me. I stood where I was and listened. And something in my mind snapped, and awoke. And for the first time, standing in a field at the age of six, in one, wild, rapturous act of reasoned reflection, I knew that I had a mother! I knew that she was young, and was beautiful, and was my own. I knew that it was her business—and had been hitherto, though I had not consciously noticed it—to feed me, clothe me, and spend her life in my service. I knew that she worked too hard. I knew that she hated to call through the open window in this fashion and to make herself conspicuous for the open gossip of the street, for she had great pride. I also knew with a startling realization, hitherto unappreciated, that we were poor. Pudding was only a piece of stale cake with sauce on it, yet this was to be my reward or punishment. Pudding for the poor!

These were the apocalypses of my early childhood.

GENTLEMAN WITH A GRUDGE

UPON ATTAINING the use of reason in a positive and permanent form, I found that among seasons, summer was most to my liking. During my favorite months—the hot ones—I used to don a pair of overalls and a farm-boy's hat, and plucking a blade of grass on which to chew, would go wandering in our neighborhood so as to explore its houses and inhabitants by way of discovering what sort of world it was I had come to live in.

A favorite rendezvous of mine was a nearby shop which aspired to be a general store in a very small way. This shop had only one window and a little side entrance, and exteriorly it gave the impression of being a fruit store, for there were always oranges and bananas exposed for sale at the door. But inside, it proved to be a bit of everything. It was a grocery shop if you had forgotten to order a can of peas; it was a bakeshop if you needed a sudden loaf of bread; it had a plaything department selling tops and marbles for boys' games; and it would do for a drug store if you needed liniment or iodine in an emergency. It always seemed to me to be a brave little shop, trying to be all these things at once. It was open days and nights, and even Sunday mornings.

The full-fledged fruit shops of our town were exclusively in the hands of the Italians, but this amateur fruit shop was owned by a Yankee. He was a tall man, with loose-fitting clothes, a walrus moustache, and spectacles, and his name was one of those odd Yankee names that so amuse the Irish, a name in which the syllables are words and give you a strange association of ideas, like Frothingham, Saltonstall, Winterbottom. The proprietor's name was Wigglesworth.

Though I had read no Dickens at the time I first met Mr. Wigglesworth, once I had gone through David Copperfield and Nicholas Nickleby, I knew that he was definitely a Dickens character. For he had that odd quality which a Dickens character can display, of being sufficiently crazy to amuse you, without being sufficiently dangerous to do you any harm. Mr. Wigglesworth's mild dementia was revealed in his fondness for making speeches to an audience of one. If the audience happened to be only one small boy, but lately possessed of the use of reason, it made no difference to Mr. Wigglesworth. He went right on orating in adult language as though addressing the Senate or the House of Representatives. He would discourse on war, on politics, on marriage, on literature, on anything that supplied him with enthusiasm. He liked especially to air his grudges, his grudges against life in general and particular, to tell what was wrong with men and their affairs, and how it could be corrected. One of his chief grudges was the bad fruit Americans are given to eat.

"The United States," Mr. Wigglesworth once said to me as I sat on one of his onion crates, chewing a straw, "the United States, my boy, is a nation of unripe bananas!"

While saying this, he made a most contemptuous gesture toward the front door of his establishment, by way of indicating that his own bananas, hanging on a stalk there, were included in the censure.

"Yes, sir!" Mr. Wigglesworth repeated, because he always repeated anything that seemed to him like a weighty pronouncement, "this is a nation of unripe bananas!"

"Is it?" I said.

"Is it!" Mr. Wigglesworth replied, because he always repeated you as well as himself, "Good God, did you ever see the things the way they ship them to us from South America?"

"No, sir."

"No, sir? Well, you ought to! They're absolutely green, my boy, so green and hard you couldn't crack one with a rock. Imagine a banana taken off the tree in that condition!"

I at once closed my eyes, and endeavored to visualize the fruit interiorly, and to appreciate its horrible state.

"Bananas, my boy," Mr. Wigglesworth then went on, having sensed that he had begun to impress me, "should be left on the tree until they are *ripe!*"—and he would rip off the word as though snapping a whip—"not torn off the tree while they are *green!* put in a cellar till they become *yellow!* and hung up for sale until they become *rotten!* Do you see what I mean?" and he made an odd gesture of futility, like a scarecrow gyrating in a storm.

I assured him that I was *trying* to see what he meant, and then sat quietly and awaited further developments of a theme upon which I knew he would be glad to expatiate.

Having refreshed his mouth, inside with a bite of tobacco, and outside with a rub from a red handkerchief, and having adjusted his collar so as to give more comfort to the throat, Mr. Wigglesworth continued.

"There isn't a single person in the forty-eight States of this Union, my boy—excepting someone who has travelled to South America, like myself—who has ever tasted the flavor of a real ripe banana, a golden banana that has been left on the tree for the sun to work on, to mellow it and bring it to maturity, with a full rich flavor, and a firm brown skin. No, sir, there's not a person in this country that knows what a banana like that tastes like. They either eat green bananas, and that gives them appendicitis; or else they eat rotten bananas, and that gives them dysentery. Now which will you take?"

I said I thought I should take the second, if forced to a choice.

"What!" Mr. Wigglesworth shrieked out, "You would?" And then a sudden reserve which all adults arrive at eventually when they are dealing with children, restrained him. He looked at me with a hesitant regard, and knew immediately two things: first, that I did not know what the disease he had mentioned was; and second, that it was well for me not to know. Children catch these flashes of caution in the conversation of their elders with unerring accuracy. That is why it is foolish for a grown-up to answer all the questions of a child.

One could not fail, however, to admire Mr. Wigglesworth's consistency and sincerity when dealing with his customers. If, in the course of one of his banana harangues, a lady customer should enter the shop to buy bananas, Mr. Wigglesworth's strong aversions concerning the unsuitability of that fruit for human consumption would not in the least diminish.

"Which do you want?" he would say to the woman, "that yellow bunch, which is unripe, or that spotted bunch, which is rotten?"

This disarming frankness on the part of her tradesman would seem to give the woman only more confidence in Mr. Wigglesworth and his wares. She would order the unripe ones, or the rotten ones, as the case might be, then pay him the price, and depart cheerfully. Mr. Wigglesworth would then clink a cash drawer with a bell attached to it, deposit the dishonest money therein, slam the drawer until it closed again, and continue to be thoroughly disgusted with his profession.

"What can I do, my boy?" Mr. Wigglesworth would muse, as he surveyed the woman he had cheated, while she went waddling down the street, "I give them advice, but they won't take it! But I repeat, the United States is a nation of unripe bananas!"

"Or else rotten ones, Mr. Wigglesworth!" I would add.

"You're right, son!" Mr. Wigglesworth would say, as he patted me on the head, for he loved one who would agree with him, "Or else rotten ones!" And there the subject might end for the moment.

I have said that Mr. Wigglesworth liked you when you agreed with him. But with all the good will in the world, it was difficult to do this consistently. For he had the habit of planting false leads in his conversation which made the trend of his thought difficult to follow, and threw his listener completely off the track. I shall give an example of what I mean.

"I see," Mr. Wigglesworth said one day, while misting and drying his spectacles, "that young Slocum's gone and got himself engaged to be married. The darn fool! That kid ain't set for marriage yet, not by a long shot. Furthermore, he ain't got any money. Furthermore, I understand the girl he's going to marry has a perfectly impossible disposition. Cranky as a rattlesnake, so I hear. That ain't no kind of a girl to marry. I fell in love with a cranky girl myself when I was young. I even went so far as to become engaged to her, before I discovered how disagreeable she was. And then do you know what I did?"

"You threw her over, Mr. Wigglesworth?"

"Nope! I married her, went right ahead and married her. Shows what a darn fool I was. Not only was she cranky, my boy, but do you know what she was? She was a hypocrite. She told me she had a thousand dollars in the bank, all her own. That's what she told me."

"And was that a lie, Mr. Wigglesworth?"

"Bless your heart, no! She had one thousand, one hundred and three dollars in the bank, all in her own name, certified to by a bank book. That's what she had. But do you know what she promised me? She promised that when we were married she would turn the whole sum of money over to me; said she would sign it all over to me just as soon as we were married. That's what she promised."

"But she didn't do it, Mr. Wigglesworth?"

"Didn't do it? I'll tell you she did. Every darn cent of it. She signed on the dotted line the day after the minister hitched us. But that ain't what I'm comin' to. What I'm comin' to, son, is this. Do you know what that woman, that woman with the cranky disposition, whom I married through sheer pity, do you know what she went around sayin' about me after we were married? She went around sayin' that I married her for her money! That's what she said. Good God, what can you do with a woman like that?"

I was not able to answer this last question. But it echoed a thought that was already simmering in my own mind. I had already heard of a lady who drank "kerosene oil" for asthma. Now I had met a man who hated bananas and was being falsely accused by his wife. It set me believing at an early age that human existence was bound to be full of such alarms and disappointments.

Mr. Wigglesworth passed out of my life as casually as he had entered it. I can go back to my native city and locate the shop where I first met him, but it is no longer the shop of Mr. Wigglesworth's day and mine. It is now a large establishment, with two windows instead of one, and with a door for entrance at the center, and is owned by a chain-store grocery company.

One feature of Mr. Wigglesworth's companionship I shall always be grateful for. He never spoke to me as though it were necessary for me to be stupid by way of being young. He spoke to me always as though I had intelligence, intelligence which needed to be guided in many points, and supplied with a vocabulary in others, but intelligence none the less. This is the greatest compliment a child can receive. As a child I always hated to be talked down to. I hated all nursery nonsense directed towards my ears. I hated in every way to be babied. I particularly hated to have things over-explained to me. Mr. Wigglesworth never treated me as though I were a dunce. He treated me as though I were a man, and that's what I liked, and was the reason why I visited him wearing a laborer's overalls, and chewing a conversational straw.

Whether or not Mr. Wigglesworth died with his antipathy for bananas still unabated, I do not know. I thought of him particularly after the first World War when the popular song was being sung: "Yes, we have no bananas!" I thought how much Mr. Wigglesworth, if he lived, would have rejoiced in that song.

DESIGN FOR A GRECIAN URN

To GIVE my father credit, when he found he had some children on his hands, he decided to go out and do something about it in the matter of finances. Having carefully analyzed the likes and dislikes of his children (we were ultimately three boys and one girl), partially by listening to their prattle, partially by receiving reports thereon from the neighbors, he made up his mind that we needed luxuries to go with our fantastic imaginations, and he was determined to supply them.

Perhaps one of the reasons why I could never rouse myself to a Communist's rage against what has been lately called the Capitalistic System, or the Republican Rule, is because it was possible under such a system or rule for a poor boy with energy and ability to rise from a state of poverty to one of practical comfort bordering on wealth.

My father gave up working in a shoe factory and joined the forces of a life insurance company. In no time he was raised from the status of agent to that of assistant manager, and thence to the post of manager and given the running of a large office with five or six stenographers and more than forty men under him. In a single season he produced more business for his company than any other manager in the United States and Canada. He was invited to New York to attend a great banquet, and sat next to the President of the Company.

I always feel very proud of my father on that occasion, sitting next to the President, wearing the light blue tie my mother had given him, instead of the stiff black one of formal dress, and letting the officers of the largest life insurance company in the world know that it isn't decoration that makes the hero. I learned from other sources that my father impressed all present on that occasion, for he had youth and considerable charm.

My father had great shrewdness in business. Life insurance, at the time when my father was making his company famous, was suspect in many quarters. It seemed to many like a silly investment of money in case you didn't die quickly and cash in on the investment. I once heard my father say to a man who was abusing the notion of life insurance in general: "What are you talking about? You couldn't get any life insurance, anyhow!"

"Why not?" said the man.

"Because you have cirrhosis of the liver. No company would take you."

This worried the man, and he called on my father a few days later to see if my father had meant what he said.

"Well, let us go over to our medical examiner and have him look you over and see," said my father, and they both went.

The medical examiner found the man's liver in excellent condition, and this so pleased the man that he let my father write him up for a ten thousand dollar policy. The man insisted that the joke was on my father. He slapped my father on the back and shouted: "You see! You were wrong!" And, of course, my father had to admit that he was.

My father, when addressing his agents in their weekly meeting, told of this incident, and reminded them that it was a good idea at times to give people the impression that they can't get a thing, so as to make them want it all the more.

At the next meeting of the office force, one of my father's agents came in with a black eye.

"Where did you get that eye?" my father asked him.

"From putting your business principles into practice," said the agent; "I told a man who said he didn't believe in insurance that he couldn't get any because he was sick. And he said: 'Oh, I am, am I?'"

When my father's income reached the stage where it supplied him with a satisfactory bank account, he undertook to supply his children (a) with the best of educations, and that in a Sisters' school where each of us was exposed for nine years to the lovely radiance and elegant manners of Catholic nuns; (b) with a training in music; I was apprenticed to the violin which twisted my neck and gave me astigmatism; my second brother was assigned to the clarinet, which nearly blew out his ears; my sister took up singing, and sings beautifully to this day; while my youngest brother espoused the piano, and has since forgotten all he learned; (c) with the best of vacations in the summer time.

Being sea urchins, practically born on the beach, my father

thought it nice for us to spend our vacations in the country. He secured a boarding house for us, which was almost a hotel, in the New Hampshire hills, not far from the foot of Mt. Kearsage, and equidistant from the shores of Lake Sunapee. Thither we excursioned for at least three weeks each summer so as to see how good it was to be away from the ocean, and so as to appreciate it better on our return.

Our host and hostess were twangy New Hampshire farmers who specialized in home-like courtesy and good food. Their conversation was full of that rustic wisdom and native wit which needs to be savored in actual experience to know how delicious it can be. We enjoyed these vacations, but I remember them particularly by reason of a little girl who stayed one summer at our inn, a little girl whose name I never learned and never shall, but who enchanted me while listening to her half hour of practice on the piano every morning at nine. She began with fifteen minutes of scales, and ended with fifteen minutes of attempted Chopin. Maybe it was Madame Chaminade who was the composer, but I think it was Chopin, in one of the Preludes. I was as faithful in attending these practice sessions as the little girl was. I knew exactly when she was to begin. There was a circular staircase descending from the second floor to the music room. And every morning found me seated on the stairs, listening to her while she played.

There is a moment in Art (and in Life too, where it approximates the ideal state of Art) which may be variously described as the inchoative moment, the moment of poise or suspense, the moment of the sustained instant. It is the artist's brave, hopeless attempt to fix the present, by denying it a future, so as to refuse it a past. Lessing speaks in his Laocoön of "the extended stationary object" required for a painting, that supreme moment of magic when all the figures are poised for action. Picasso said to Gertrude Stein after he had painted her portrait "It doesn't look like you, Gertrude, but it will!" The peasants in Millet's Angelus are always *on the point of making* the Sign of the Cross. Cellini's Head of Perseus is always *about to drip* blood. Leonardo da Vinci's Mona Lisa is forever *on the verge* of smiling. Were La Gioconda ever once to open her lips and laugh, that, my dears, would be the end of art! . . . What I speak of is also the theme of a poem, Keats' "Ode on a Grecian Urn," where the heifers and the maids with garlands are always *going to the fair*.

I once read a story about a rich family who had erected on their estate a beautiful sunken garden and filled it with objects of art. There was a stone hound, about to run in the chase. There was a stone archer, about to shoot a bow. There was a stone lady, about to eat a bunch of grapes. The rich family exhibited the garden once—that, in a large week-end party to their friends—and then went off to Europe and left it. In their absence they made no provision for the care of the garden. The fountain dried up. The flowers in the urns decayed. The benches were overgrown with weeds. And the statuaries became covered with cobwebs. These granite beauties, angered at being so disregarded, held a conspiracy one moonlight night. They resolved to undo themselves as objects of art. The lady ate the grapes. The archer shot the bow. The dog ran away. Thus did they avenge themselves on the unappreciative rich family who owned them.

It was such a moment of sustained suspense that existed between me and the little girl who played the piano in the summer boarding-house near Lake Sunapee. Precisely at nine o'clock each morning I would come and sit on the stairs (the seventh step from the top, if I remember) and resting my elbows on my knees and my chin in my hands, would listen for the half hour of her practice. Precisely at nine o'clock she would enter the guests' parlor, and twirling the piano stool till she could both sit on it and touch her toes to the floor, and suitably arranging herself in other ways, would begin her scales, to be followed by the incipient phrases of the Chopin

Prelude. Not for all the kingdoms of the world would she turn her head to look at me. Not for all the kingdoms of the world would I descend one further step on the stairs. She knew that I was listening to her, and I knew that she knew it. And she knew that I knew that she knew. It was a perfect collaboration in a perfect ruse between two strange children, too shy to be playmates, too immature to be lovers, too young to be disillusioned, too old to be deceived.

We both knew that it was part of the requirement for preserving this haunting half hour that we should be inconspicuous to each other for the rest of the day. I never knew where she went when her lesson was over. She never saw me except at mealtimes. I never spoke to her. Neither learned the other's name. At the end of a fortnight she departed with her parents to mix with the maelstrom of common life and be carried on in its relentless tide. We never met again.

But she has lingered with me always in the manner of a dream and often returns to me as a symbol. Whenever I have been seated in a theatre and the house lights were lowered and the curtain about to rise; whenever I have watched a symphony conductor raise his baton for the first down-beat that will release a great splurge of music; when I have stood on the threshold of the Pitti Palace about to gaze at the wonders, or shaded my eyes to enter the cathedrals of Milan and Cologne, or peered for the first time from the balcony of the Hôtel des Invalides, to catch a glimpse of the little casket of Napoleon; at every pent-up moment of my life when I have waited for some artistic surprise to flash before my senses, there has come back to me the vision of a little girl in the hills of New Hampshire about to strike her first chord on the piano during that fortnight of magical summer mornings, at the precise hour of nine, when she was contemplatively mine.

What became of her, I do not know. I doubt not that life has dealt roughly with her, as it does with all precious things. But I like to think that I am unforgotten in her memories as she is in mine, and that amidst the stale platitudes that serve her for comfort in the fatigues and yawns of middle age, one bright picture lingers with her still: that of a boy who was content to admire her for her music, and sat like a sculpture and listened like a painting, at a point on the staircase that was half way down the stairs.

SUNDAY EVENINGS

OUR HOUSE was always ablaze on Sunday evenings. We invariably had at least three roomsful of visitors, and what with music, laughter and oratory, I do not know what the neighbors thought of us. It must have seemed as if the Feeneys were putting on a perpetual bazaar. As far as I can remember we never visited anybody. People always visited us.

If we are bankrupt today—and we nearly are—it was my father's gargantuan sense of hospitality that is responsible. The first thing my father asked you when he met you in our home was to stay all night. My mother needed continually to keep extra food on hand against the sudden overnight invitations issued by my father to guests who had merely dropped in to say Hello. If you came from out of town, it was absolutely impossible to get away from us. I have often got up in the morning, and peeking into our spare rooms on the way down to breakfast, found sleeping in our beds people I never knew existed. Our borrowed-pajama bill was enormous.

We domesticated at different periods at least a dozen of our relatives, and they lived with us until they either (a) died, (b) married, or (c) entered religion.

My father was an incorrigible cenobite. He detested solitude and had a positive horror of silence. He delighted in noise in any form. He particularly liked to hear others sing. The worse

you sang the more my father applauded, and the more he
urged you to an encore. He had an extreme fondness for the
noises made by musical instruments. There was McCarthy who
came with his clarinets, and would squeal on them till two in
the morning, but never too long for my father. There was
Clancy who played marathons on the violin.

Clancy was an ex-tinker from Ireland. His family was a
troupe of musicians and Clancy was born out of doors at
one of the crossroad fairs. He claimed to have ten thousand
tunes in his head, and it seemed to be my father's greatest
ambition to hear every one of them before Clancy's nimble
fingers succumbed to arthritis. I have known Clancy to play
continuously for a stretch of six hours in our parlor, and to be
fed by my father while he played. However, I must say that
Clancy was worth listening to. He had the most delicate sense
of cadenza I have ever heard on a stringed instrument, and
could pizzicato like nobody's business.

Yet for all his virtuosity, Clancy was shy in his art, and
needed to be coaxed into a performance. I have seen him sulk
through a whole Sunday evening, refusing to play a note.
This would invariably happen if there were a single person in
our parlor whom Clancy disliked. Hostility of any kind petri-
fied him, for he was sensitive in the manner of great genius.
My father hit upon a nearly infallible device for getting
Clancy to play when he was disinclined to. It was to take up
the violin himself and saw a few notes on it badly. Then my
father would give a feeble imitation of Clancy himself, playing one of his favorite hornpipes. This would amuse Clancy
enormously, but after one bad round of the hornpipe by my
father, Clancy would begin to fidget, and commence lighting
and relighting his pipe. He would twist nervously in his chair
and wince at every note misplayed by my father. Finally, un-
able to stand it any longer, he would shout: "Give me that
thing, Tom!" He would then wrest the fiddle out of my
father's hands, retune it to his own desires, limber his fingers

with a few scales and flourishes, and then he was away on his own. And he might never stop until the milkman arrived in the morning.

When there were no musicians or orators around, my father would read—by which I mean to say, he would read out loud. Nothing suited my father better than a spell of quiet among the company while he recited "Robert Emmet's Speech from the Dock," or one of the political orations of Senator Jim Reed. If a crowd were lacking, one person would do, provided he would let my father read to him. The auditor need not necessarily listen, as long as he kept quiet and did not interrupt my father. I have known my father to read the whole of Enoch Arden to Guy Pelosi, an Italian tailor, to whom every line of the poem was unintelligible. Pelosi had merely sauntered in to gather some pants to be pressed, but my father took the afternoon off to treat him to Tennyson and the extensive art of narrative poetry. Pelosi was very fond of my father, secretly believing him to be an Italian in disguise, and patiently listened to yards and yards of English literature dramatically delivered to him by my father's voice. "Your father has a darn gooda voice" was Pelosi's invariable comment when my father had polished him off with an epic or two. This poetic influence of my father on his friend, Pelosi, was bound to be felt, and my father keeps in his scrap book one of the cards Pelosi issued in advertisement of his trade. It is written entirely in verse, and runs as follows:

Read this from beginning to end,
And you'll find out I'm your good friend.
If you wish to know my nationality
I came from Italy.
From the time I left Naples City,
After twelve days I reached New York Liberty
I began to get acquainted in this country,
And I found the people in the shade of the apple tree.

Everybody treated me kind
Now, don't leave me behind,
Don't be sorry to come and see me,
I'll give you first-class fit and good quality,
If I make you a suit
Among your friends
You will look like a beautiful posy
And I am Yours Truly, Guy Pelosi

I have a suspicion that my father helped Pelosi in the composition of this poem, but my father says "No," and Pelosi refuses to answer.

The number and range and quality of our callers on Sunday evenings was prodigious. We have had guests from Nova Scotia, Central America and the Aleutian Islands. We knew a heavyweight wrestler, a symphony conductor, a roller-skating champion, and an ex-end man in Lew Dockstader's minstrels. I have counted in our parlor at a single sitting, a ventriloquist, a magician, an impersonator of animals, and a lady who told fortunes with the assistance of tea leaves.

My father's chief office as host was to get everyone to perform, whether by way of musical instrument, in song, or in telling a story. My father believed solemnly in the Parable of the Talents. If you had only One Talent my father would find it, though you buried it in a napkin and hid it in the ground. My father was a splendid interlocutor, and few could resist him. My father had contempt for only one vice, and that was timidity. "Oh, what's the matter with you!" he would say if you positively refused to contribute anything to the general amusement by way of song or recitation. My father, who is the most charitable man I have ever known, had one supreme condemnation: "He's got no gumption!" It was the worst and only thing I ever heard my father say in dispraise of anyone.

So if you hadn't any gumption, Feeneys' on Sunday nights was the wrong place for you to go to. The fact that practically nobody we knew ever stayed away, is probably a proof that gumption had been rather largely distributed among our friends. Of course my father's interpretation of the Parable of the Talents was, in the strict sense, open to criticism. You might have talent for other things besides songs and stories, and yet not fall under the censure of Our Saviour. But "talent" to my father, meant talent for entertaining. It meant that and nothing more.

How my father could be wrong, I propose to show in the case of one of our best loved friends.

The same was Mary's Joe. Mary was the wife, and Joe the husband. There were many Marys and many Joes among our callers and acquaintances, but there was only one "Mary and Joe." "Joe's Mary" or "Mary's Joe" would serve to identify either of them in complete contradistinction to any others who had poached on the same names. And if you were referring to an incident that happened in their home, you would say that it happened "up at Mary and Joe's."

Mary and Joe were as opposite in disposition, temperament, taste, as any two persons could possibly be. She was all feminine, he was all man. It was their hardship that they were childless.

Joe was a plumber. Mary, who was given to euphemisms in his regard, used to call him "an expert mechanic." But we knew he was a plain plumber, and loved him none the less for it. At any rate, among our incorrigible visitors, among those who were practically fixtures at every Sunday evening party —so much so that if they didn't come, we called them on the telephone to ask what was wrong—were Mary and Joe.

Mary had talent, in my father's sense. She could sing, she could clown, she could tell a joke. But Joe had none. Histrionically he was a complete flop. All he could do at our gatherings was sit and listen. My father tried to prod him into action for the first two or three years of our acquaintanceship, but finally gave him up as hopeless. "Joe has absolutely no gumption!" my father decided, and even Mary was forced to agree.

So there he sat, Sunday evening after Sunday evening, the strong, silent Joe, always taking the most uncomfortable chair, always getting up to give his seat to another, always carrying in furniture to supply repose where it was needed, always getting out of somebody else's way. "I know I have no gumption!" I once heard him say; "Your father's right! But what can I do about it?"

Yet there were many things Joe could do in other fields besides that of entertainment. He was the spare godfather for everybody's baby, the spare pallbearer at everybody's funeral. That is to say, if the godfather or pallbearer you had chosen didn't show up at christening or wake, then, as the saying amongst us went, "You could always get Joe."

Joe was a particular favorite of my mother's. My mother was always saying that Joe had depths in him that nobody had sounded, qualities that nobody had appreciated. Joe, in turn, fairly worshipped my mother, and said boldly in the presence of his wife that my mother was the most beautiful woman he had ever seen. In one of my mother's illnesses Joe used to come to her sickroom, and just sit there and look at her for hours, never saying a word. He was always at my mother's beck and call on Sunday nights. If something were lacking in the collation my mother was preparing, and someone were needed to run out to the store, Joe was invariably the messenger for that. There was hardly a Sunday night when we did not hear him say "Here's your change, Mrs. Feeney!" as he returned from an errand, and then deposited himself in silence in some distant chair, to gaze in wonderment at the general entertainment.

Joe was also a great favorite with us children. He was always quietly listening to things we had to tell him, always quietly approving of what we had to say. It was not possible for us to read his eyes then as we could read them now, and perhaps fortunate as well. For there is a hunger in the eyes of a childless husband—a bewilderment, a sense of defeat with no explanation—that would wreck the heart of every child he looks at, were it other than the heart of a child.

Mary went out of her way, so to speak, to compensate for Joe. Whereas he told no stories, she told an extra one in his stead. Whereas he laughed little, and that always undemonstratively, she roared to the point of slapping others on the back. Whereas he used bad English when he spoke at all, she polished up hers to suit the queen's taste, and dealt it out in interminable chatter.

There was one point in which Mary and Joe perfectly complemented each other. He was healthy, and she was unwell. It was not until a number of years had passed that her illness became tragic, but when it did, it became tragic indeed. She contracted the various diseases a woman, as woman, can be heir to. She was confined to her bed for years. Her fundamental ailment was put down in that most exasperating of all diagnoses: *nervousness!* And what can you do about that?

Joe waited on Mary hand and foot. He cooked the meals, washed the linen, scrubbed the floor. He paid countless doctor's bills. He sat by her bedside endeavoring by every device he could employ to calm her excitement, to quiet her hysterical fears. She drooped one night, and died in his arms.

But I like to think of them most in the years before this catastrophe, when they were younger, more hopeful, when it was Sunday evening and they were ours; when almost the very first ring of the front door bell was a signal for one of us to say "Ah! I'll bet that's Mary and Joe." And it very nearly always was!

I should like particularly to tell of the one night of triumph Joe enjoyed at our home, a night that was his so manifestly that not even Mary could enhance it by crowing about it or exaggerating its importance.

We were all gathered together one memorable Sunday evening. Our parlor and dining room were full. Andrew Philip

Pumford Dunk, from Glasgow, was giving us Scotch jokes
and imitations of Harry Lauder. Tom Murray, a tenor, built
like a bass, was rendering the pitiable strains of "Mona" a lady
who, it seems, died and left somebody lonely after her. John Z.
Kelley, chief soloist in our parish choir, had just finished one
of his beautiful Ave Marias. He alternated between Gounod's
and Schubert's with a slight preference for the latter. My
mother had served an excellent collation, and in the periods of
respite for eating and conversation, my father was winding the
victrola. When suddenly we heard the sound of a big wind,
blowing in the distance.

"Phew!" said somebody, while munching a sandwich,
"sounds like a storm beginning!"

Louder and louder the wind blew, a torrential lot of it,
bound to take off our roof if it kept on that way.

Finally the voice of our maid, who had gone to the attic to
close all the windows, was heard screaming at the top of the
stairs.

"Mrs. Feeney! Mrs. Feeney! The pipe has burst in the bathroom, and it's flooding the place with water! It's running down
through the floor, Mrs. Feeney, and it's ruining the ceiling in
the kitchen!"

The fun stopped suddenly, and there was a great hush, while
we listened to the falling water. Each of us looked at the other
in consternation. Then all eyes turned to Joe. This was no
moment for a nit-wit entertainer. This was the time we needed
a plumber, and a plumber, thank God, we had!

Joe arose quietly and took off his coat. He was masterful in
the way he assumed command. All decisions must be made like
lightning, and like lightning his were made. Where did he rush
to? To the bathroom, to see what was going on? Not Joe. But
to the cellar, where never a Feeney would have ever thought
of going.

"Have you got a candle?"

My mother had one.

"Do you know where the main line comes in?"

My mother didn't know.

"Doesn't Mr. Feeney?"

"Oh, Heavens, no!"

"Well, we've got to find it!"

And candle ahead, we all went traipsing down to the cellar, with Joe leading us.

Quietly he surveyed the pipes, made a conjecture, and found it correct. Then down on all fours, disregardful of Sunday clothes, crawling amidst the coal, the cobwebs, the footprints of the cats, he found the necessary valve. It was rusty and would not turn. Not for one of us. But it would for Joe. He would *make* it turn! . . . Ugh! Ugh! Ugh! . . . Twist! Twist! Twist! . . . Turn! Turn! Turn! . . . Ugh! Ugh! Ugh! "One more'll get it! There! . . . That'll hold the water for awhile! Now let us go up stairs for the repair."

We were absolutely wide-eyed in admiration. Every action was a masterpiece. Even to the way he plugged the broken pipe with cork and rags until it could be soldered with lead in the morning.

A half an hour later found Joe seated placidly in the kitchen, being served hot tea by my mother, and wearing one of my father's shirts.

About once a year my mother refers to my father as "Mr. Feeney," by way of re-surveying the man she married.

"Mr. Feeney couldn't have fixed that thing in a million years," was my mother's summary of our bathroom explosion. And we all knew it was a just one.

The guests departed a little earlier than usual that Sunday night, in respect for our upset nerves. You can be sure there was no further attempt at any kind of entertainment.

There was nothing to talk about while our friends were leaving except Joe, and how wonderful he was.

Mary epitomized our praise with a triumphant twinkle in her eye. "No gumption, eh?" was what the twinkle kept saying. And she led her husband by the arm to the door.

My father watched them descending the front steps.

And then Mr. Feeney went back and turned off the victrola.

LESSON FROM THE LITTLE MOSQUITO

MY FAVORITE word is "little." At least I use it more than I do other words. It occurs so frequently in my earlier work that I have been tempted to go back and delete it here and there. It occurs in the title of one of my books: "In Towns and Little Towns"; in the titles of many of my poems, such as "The Little Kingdom of Thingdom"; and in the titles of several of my sketches: "My Little Minister" and "This Little Thing." In the writing of my biography of Mother Seton, called "An American Woman," I resort to the word "little" so often that it is practically an impediment in my speech. One of my critics was quick to notice this and sent me a devastating parody of my own style, which ran as follows:

"Dear little Leonard Feeney. I read your little book on America's first little sisters-school nun, little Mother Seton. I think she is the nicest little nun I have ever read about, and you do say the most charming little things in her praise. Won't you please write us other little books on kindred little subjects, so as to make our little hearts a little more happy?"

A man can survive such ridicule only with the aid of prayer.

Another of my critics, a married lady, writing in one of the weekly reviews, scores not only the frequency of the word "little" in my vocabulary but its essential inappropriateness to some of my ideas. "The author," she says of me, "refers to a nun as 'a little lady all consecrated to God,' whereas we all know that many nuns are large, impressive persons, born to command."

I did not answer this enormous matron, for I believe in free criticism; but had I, I could have defended myself to some extent.

I think that "little" is definitely a Catholic epithet, used not in a dimensional, but in an appropriative sense. We call anything little that we like so much we want to make it small enough to consider it our own. There is an order of nuns in the Church known, one and all, as The Little Sisters of the Poor. But they do not weigh their postulants before receiving, nor send them reducing exercises so as to establish vocations. Our Lord speaks of the whole Church as His "little flock." Saint Francis of Assisi is known as "The Little Poor Man," and Saint Thérèse of Lisieux as "The Little Flower." Even Saint Ignatius, perhaps given to diminutives least of all the Saints, refers to the regiment of his spiritual soldiers as "this little Society of Jesus."

I have a further propensity for the word "little," because it is mostly in small things that I am largely interested. Had I become a scientist, I should have been an astronomer among the biologists, with microscope for telescope, peering into worlds beneath me, studying my heavens upside down.

At any rate, I think that not even the most captious of my critics will object to the word "little" as applied to a mosquito.

Of all the world of little things a mosquito makes the loudest noise. If you, proportionate to your weight, could make as loud a noise singing, as he does, proportionate to his when he whines, you would sound like all the factory whistles of Bethlehem Steel going off in a simultaneous blast. You would literally blow the roof off.

I first became acquainted with the little mosquito (he always seems to be the *same* mosquito) when I was a little boy lying in bed. First I shall tell you what he did to me harmfully, and then what he did to me by way of help.

By way of harm, he cost my father hundreds of dollars. It was the summer I contracted malaria and was quarantined for three months. This malaria was the work of one mosquito. He * raised my temperature five degrees, and sent me into such a series of fevers and chills that our neighbors, alarmed at my plight, and fearing contagion, would not let their children admit to ever having known me.

This same mosquito caused my mother to invest in innumerable hot water bottles and in at least a thousand pounds of ice. I wore out two ice men in the course of the summer.

My parents went scurrying to neighboring stores to purchase soups and broths of such exotic kinds and flavors that the grocers advised my mother to buy her canned goods wholesale.

Still the work of one mosquito.

And what he did to me by way of upsetting my environment was nothing to what he did to me inside my head.

Have you ever seen an elephant uproot Bunker Hill Monument and hurl it like a javelin across East Boston Harbor? . . . Well, I did, thanks to one little mosquito.

Were you ever lost for a thousand years in a dark, lonely forest, and did you eat lobsters with a giant who had street-lamps for eyes? . . . Then you never met the mosquito I met.

Were you ever, in a delirium, the only being in existence, without father or mother or friend or any one to know you or love you; with your whole body seething like a furnace, your head a conflagration of distorted ideas, your soul cindered down to the last ash, your will clinging to the last remnants of religion . . . calling to God, to Mary, to Jesus, to come and either deliver or destroy you, asking where everyone was but yourself, promising never again to be naughty . . . if only, if only, if only, if only, you could have ice on your forehead, ice on your feet, ice to hold, ice to listen to, ice to eat . . . ?

* The scientists tell me it is the female mosquito, not the male, that carries disease germs. But I prefer, chivalrously, to blame it on the male.

Do you wonder that the subject of the mosquito impresses me, and that I dedicate to it a chapter from the pages of my youth?

The little mosquito is hatched in the afternoon, in the warmth of a pleasant swamp.

Ten minutes later he is a finished aviator, ready for flight.

He is merely a bit of gauze informed with animation, and so delicate you could not weigh him on a pharmacist's scale. Yet he knows to a nicety all the currents of air and can balance himself skillfully in the most formidable breeze.

After less than an hour of personal tuning, he begins a flight more remarkable than Lindbergh's. He sails to the nearest dwellinghouse to await the retirement of the sleeper. Disregarding the basement and the bedless lower floors, he finds the sleeping-chamber and the slumbering little boy.

Daintily he alights on some susceptible part of the body, and studies carefully the mechanics of the operation. He braces himself solidly, summons all his strength, and inserts his dagger accurately in a narrow little pore.

He deposits his poison, and extracts his toll of blood.

He makes another take-off, whining contentedly, and is wafted by the wind to his sources in the swamp.

By midnight he is the father of a hundred little mosquitoes, who will follow on the morrow the example of their sire.

It is an astounding performance.

It is one of the most remarkable feats in the history of the world.

WING LEE, HAND LAUNDRY

OUR STREET was intended to be purely a residential one. But the owner of a vacant lot directly opposite our house grew tired of paying taxes on property that yielded him no revenue.

And so he erected two small shops on his land and rented them for business. A baker hired one of these shops, and Wing Lee, Hand Laundry, the other.

A rumble of resentment went up in our neighborhood when Wing Lee, Hand Laundry, moved in. Our neighbors were mostly Whigs, but they became Torys when ruffled in the matter of prestige. Appeals were sent to the City Ordinance Department, and even to the Mayor, to prevent Wing Lee from joining us. But the Mayflower legislators, when writing our local rules, had, by some miraculous oversight, failed to proscribe a Chinaman. The reason was simply that they had not foreseen him. And so Wing Lee, Hand Laundry, remained in our midst, by way of a yellow blunder in the Blue Laws of Massachusetts.

One can easily be mistaken in interpreting data reported by the senses, but hardly in the case of a Chinese laundry. And so it was no time until our noses knew that Wing Lee, Hand Laundry, had not only set up in our street, but was going full steam. And what is more, the bakeshop adjacent to his had an electric fan to blow off the foul air, with the result that the odors from the two establishments became so confused in the general let-off, that there were times when you did not know whether you were smelling a mince pie being scrubbed with ammonia, or a winged collar being fried in lard.

Wing Lee may have been an annoyance to our elders, but he was a revelation and a delight to us children. He was one of a wave of Chinamen who came to our shores in the early nineteen hundreds, a type highly tenacious of the exalted customs and ancient culture from which they sprang. For, unlike the Japanese—who are of a decidedly inferior civilization—the early Chinese were slow in adopting the Western manners and dress. The Japanese have always wanted to ape us. Not so the Chinese. A Japanese will be smuggled into New York one day, and the next go marching down Riverside Drive dressed like a Wall Street broker. But a Chinaman has always clung to his ancestral garments, observances, food, as long as it was humanly possible to preserve them. The later-day Chinaman has, alas, succumbed to the hammering imposed on him by life in our crowded cities, and his pig-tail, chop-sticks, baggy blouse and decorative slippers have largely gone. He has even become Joe Lee and John Lee in place of Wing Lee and Lung Foo. But a greatness has been sacrificed in these surrenders. Nothing survives in the Americanized Chinaman but his jaundiced complexion and his almond eyes.

Our Wing Lee, thank God, was an authentic Chinaman, primitive, unspoiled, dressed and mannered exactly as he would be in his ancient country. He fascinated me beyond anyone I have known in my youth. Make no mistake, I was reluctant to believe he was not an animal, for his skin was a perpetual yellow and he smiled like a chimpanzee. If he *must* be taken as human and I saw eventually that he must—then he seemed a composite of both sexes and all ages. He had a face as smooth and fresh as a boy's; he had long braided hair like a girl's; he had eyes like a doll's; but he wore a lady's blouse like your mother's and ornamental shoes like your fashionable aunt's; yet he smoked a pipe like your father, and made a noise when he talked like your grandfather being recorded on a gramophone.

I have never seen anyone so dissociated from human consolation as Wing Lee was—so inarticulate, so sad-eyed, so alone. He slept in the rear of his shop, and seemed to have no wife, no children, no relatives, not even any friends. There were times when I was prepared to believe that he even escaped having parents, though there seemed to be something logically wrong with that theory. At any rate, I asked few questions about him of those capable of instructing me. Wing Lee was my discovery, and I was determined to figure him out by myself.

Our family was one of the first to patronize Wing Lee. We sent him some collars to do. He was conveniently located just across the street, and you could bring the collars any time; you

did not have to be prompt with them as you did with our
Yankee laundryman, who would penalize you an extra week if
your wash was not ready when he arrived. Wing Lee's work
on our collars satisfied us, and we proceeded to let him do
some of our shirts. But there the matter stopped. We had a
superstition, partly religious, partly hygienic, about giving
Wing Lee any of our more personal clothing. So he saw only
the externals of our wardrobe. The rest of our things were sent
to a wash factory to be torn apart by wringers and mangled
by machines.

Oh the patience of the East! Was it not this lesson Wing
Lee was sent to teach us? Night and day he toiled, washed,
ironed, smoked, without the solace of a single friend. He had
no companions, only customers. He strengthened his morale
by humming little curious tunes, making little curious marks
on sheets of red and yellow paper, identifying merchandise
with his own private signals, keeping ledgers secret to himself
and his gods. What an assignment for a man with whom not
one of us could compete in ancestry, who had heirlooms in his
family that had descended through the ages!

Bereft of his relics, his rice fields, his tinkling temples, his
open-air pagodas, Wing Lee braved the sloppy springs, swel-
tering summers, and icy winters of New England. He piled
up his pennies against a slow return to his homeland and a burst
of riches and surprises for those he loved. He endured a decade
as though it were a day. He spoke seldom and saw all things.
Nothing interested him less than a clock. He listened without
a murmur to the angry landlord, scolding him for something
he did not understand. He bore the complaints and rebukes
of his clients, and sought always to appease them with Oriental
courtesies. He hated the mechanical contrivances employed in
the laundry trade. He washed every single item of your clothing with his own bare hands. He would have done even better
if you had put him out of doors, given him some good strong
suds and supplied him with a river. His was not the artificial

cleanliness of the Occident, but the essential cleanliness of the East, where libation is a religious ritual and every pool has been adopted by a deity.

One day, suddenly, with no warning, the sign "Wing Lee, Hand Laundry" was taken down. He vanished as silently as he came. No one knew why, or where. Was it that this great lover of silence could no longer stand our noise?

I do not know. It may be that he went to New York and drugged himself with opium in an effort to forget us. It may be that he was killed in one of the tong wars in San Francisco, still trying to put us out of his mind. But I have a suspicion that Wing Lee sailed home to China, and that he remembered us very well. I have a notion that you might find him even now in the suburbs of some metropolis, in the hills above Canton or the valleys below Peiping, chuckling to his grandchildren, patting their heads, and telling them of his days in distant Massachusetts when he laundered the dirty linen of the low-brows of Lynn.

HEAVEN IN A POND

IT WAS STRANGE being told in school by our Sisters that we were not made for this world. My grandmother's death had given me a suspicion on this point, but the nuns turned it into a certitude and made it part of our program. We were to plan for death just as much as we planned for life, and were to expect it at any moment, perhaps before we were promoted to the next grade in school. I found the predicament rather exciting: that of anticipating another world before you had quite got on to the hang of this one.

I used often to count the children in my class in the morning, and if any one was absent with a cold or a sore throat, I felt sure he had died during the night, until reassured to the contrary. If I remember correctly, only one of my classmates died in the first nine years of my attendance at school, and this did not seem to be a very good record in the face of such a universal threat. Nevertheless, in other quarters of our town, I had seen with my own eyes the undertaker arrive and pin a crêpe on the doorposts of many comparatively young people; and then, there was always the graveyard, where two easy dates and a simple problem in subtraction would give you an integer as small as four, three, two, even as small as one. So what the Sisters were prophesying for all of us, old and young, had better be taken seriously.

It might be thought that this waiting-room attitude toward the life to come would have induced us to take little interest in terrestrial surroundings so precariously ours. Quite the contrary. The psychology of the waiting-room, as those who have visited the dentist's will testify, is one of fervid interest—interest in the furniture, the wall-paper, the pictures, the magazines on the desk, even begetting in the patient an impulse to translate the Latin of the dentist's diploma. You make a minute study in a waiting-room of details you would never even notice in your own home.

But did not this thought of death persistently proposed by the Catholic ethic and philosophy have a tendency to make us morbid? This was not so either. Morbid thoughts are all too frequently the result of a morbid physical condition of the thinker. Children, with healthy appetites and good digestions, unlike their melancholy elders in the throes of liver ailments, have the happy habit of turning tremendous truths to their own gay purposes. "Take a good look around, for you won't be here long!" was death's fundamental message to me as a child. Life, when surveyed thus, became like an idea you get while whirling on a merry-go-round, waiting for the thing to stop. The thought might be dizzy, but it was certainly not drab.

Nevertheless, I was intrigued with the notion of the hereafter, once it had been suggested by my religious teachers, and I was anxious to gather as many descriptions of the celestial state as it was possible to find. Needless to say, it was not possible to find much. The hereafter proposed to us by the Sisters was in the form of Heaven. It was also, of course, proposed to us in the form of Hell. But, in the manner of perfect ladies, the Sisters supposed that their precious charges would never be so rash as to want to take any decided steps in the latter direction. Wherefore, Heaven—so the nuns graciously assumed —was to be our lot when we died; that is, if we were good, or reasonably good, or, at least, not unreasonably bad. But by way of describing Heaven, the Sisters had only this to say, relying on a quotation: "Eye hath not seen, nor ear heard, nor hath it entered into the mind of man to conceive what God hath prepared for those who love Him!" This text, it has to be admitted, was more effective as an exhortation to a good life than as a description of the reward that awaits it. Intellectually, it might rouse us to hope; but there was little or nothing in it on which to pin the imagination. I was one who liked pictures to go with my pleasant thoughts, and was loath to be stumped by a Scriptural challenge refusing me a view of Paradise until the clouds of Faith are cleared.

Any absolute picture of Heaven I knew was impossible. But were there not relative ones, glimpses, approximations one could acquire, aided with clues from the Cathechism, and the help—so it happened in my case—of a little fish pond?

There was in our town, not far from my home, a beautiful little heart-shaped basin of water known as Gold Fish Pond. It was one of the minor bounties bestowed on us by the Commissioner of Parks as a reward for giving him a good substantial vote for office in the annual Fall elections. In winter this pretty watering spot was used for skating. In summer it was used for fish; not fish to fish, but fish to contemplate, with alert attention and a roving eye.

Gold Fish Pond was the scene of innumerable summer picnics, and served as the place of regatta for the paper boats of small children. The fish with which it was stocked ranged in color from violent purple to screaming gold, and these little beauties, when tired of their orgies in the mud, would swim to the surface and leap in the air, or else nibble idly the floating crumbs and wafers distributed for their sustenance by youthful admirers.

Gold Fish Pond was a place to which one could bring fancies of all sorts, and find them reflected in patterns and designs beyond belief. It was a veritable cauldron of liquid and light, bursting with bubbles and glinting with gold. It always seemed to me like the picture of the brain of a fairy-tale maker, such as Grimm, Aesop, or Hans Andersen; or, better, the heart of one of these poets exposed for view.

At any rate, it was on the banks of Gold Fish Pond, while prostrate on hands and knees, with my nose almost touching the surface of the water, that I came to learn by analogy what Heaven was like.

Heaven, so the Catechism of Christian Doctrine declared, was a place of supernatural happiness. That meant to say, that the happiness which will be ours in eternity has no points of comparison with the happiness of this earth. For Heaven is a state of beatitude beyond the expectations, beyond the needs, beyond the normal capacities of our nature. Heaven is the substance of the great feast of existence, not a dessert added on by way of ice cream. One must not try to apprehend Heaven as a place of super-sunsets in the west, super-breezes on the lake, super-flowers in the garden. Heaven is utterly different from earth's panorama of aural and visual delights. The beauties we behold here below are only a promise of Heaven, not a portrayal: in some sense a symbol, and surely a hint, but infinitely inadequate as an illustration.

Armed with these premises, and restrained with these cautions, it was possible to make some estimate of our present condition of life in comparison with the life to come, by looking at the fish in Gold Fish Pond.

Suppose, I mused to myself, these little fish were put in this pond by way of probation. Suppose they were told by God a number of things they must do, in reward for doing which well, a heaven would be allotted to them. What would a heaven for fish be? First, naturally; that is to say, in terms of "wetter water and slimier slime."

A natural heaven for fish would be easy to construct. As a reward for serving God faithfully in a foul pond, God would put them in a fresh pond, and there let them abide. Theirs would be a "promised water" serving them in the guise of a "promised land." It would be fed with rivulets from luscious springs, sanded with clean, bright sand, foliaged with rich coral blooms, abounding in plentiful grub worms to eat. It would be unviolated by unsuitable muck, tin cans and rubbish; perpetually preserved as a museum, never utilized as a dump. There would be no hooks to molest the fish in summer, no ice to freeze them out in winter. They would never grow old, and might never die. . . . This would be a natural heaven for fish, a heaven fish could imagine, one that a mother fish might propose to her minnow, by way, let us say, of religious instruction.

But now let us suppose that the destiny of fish was to be a supernatural heaven instead of a natural one. Let us suppose that their ultimate beatitude was to surpass the barriers of a pond, and be extended to the comfortable enjoyment of the earth and air. Let us suppose that fish were destined ultimately to know the open sky in full glory, the majesty of mountains in clear view; to borrow the delights of human laughter and learning and intelligence, and to begin to romp and play like children. This would be a supernatural heaven for fish; but a heaven impossible to describe to them while they were still below the surface of the pond. For how can you describe a child in terms of a grub worm, laughter in terms of a soggy gurgle, or starlight in terms of mud?

It is the same way with us, I said to myself. We are like fish in a pond. Heaven cannot be described to us because it is "life beyond the top of the pond!" But it is as much more beautiful than this life, as ours is above the life of these poor little creatures diving in the waters.

There were many who came to Gold Fish Pond in the days of my childhood. The young came for recreation, the youths and maidens for courtship, the old for reflection. I liked often to be found among the old, and to sit with them in their silences, and undisturbed by noisy play, to make a submarine meditation and think the thoughts I was thinking.

ALICIA

SOME of my readers will feel that in the last chapter the philosopher (or shall we say the poet) got ahead of the child. This I do not admit.

In an autobiography, it is not the adult analysis of childhood impressions that counts; it is the quality and receptivity of mind existing in the child when the impressions were first received; else, how explain what a child remembers from an age when he needed to be reminded of nearly everything?

I know no childhood except my own, and can take stock of no other. I did not go around in childhood like a freak reporter interviewing other children, by way of ascertaining what it was like to be one of them.

Knowledge at all stages depends to no small degree on character. In life, early or late, we come to know what we want to know. There is an intimate connection between growth of mind and generosity of will. We remain perpetually ignorant of truths we are not disposed to receive. Wisdom is a virtue deserving high merit in Heaven, not merely a semester-report deserving high marks in school. Grace, likewise, is the signature of self on one's surroundings. No one can be taught how to be charming, nor made original by environment.

The rough draught of character is completely drawn, I believe, at ten. Hence, it is important that the child be taken seriously, even by his older self. Personality after the first decade is a matter of adding the proper details to a finished blueprint. Virtue will inevitably follow the strokes of an original moral design, and vice will be a matter for suitable erasure of inharmonious lines.

One gets few, if any, new ideas after ten, only fuller information. Likewise, one acquires no radically new habits after ten, only new motives and further example. Habits acquired after ten (the age is arbitrary, but I use it to indicate roughly the period of the parent and the primary school) superimpose themselves on the old like spirals of new wood around the central oak. If the pattern is not kept, if there is too much of a quarrel between the layers of development, the oak cracks, and the person explodes in a psychosis.

Expression is only a by-product of thought, and maturity of vocabulary does not re-originate an idea, only re-phrases it. I was able to say at ten with a gesture what I cannot express at forty, though armed with the arsenal of the dictionary. Shall I be accused of telling a false tale now, simply because I express it worse than I did thirty years ago?

There are thoughts that lie too deep for tears. There must indeed be thoughts that lie too deep for ink. Ink will do as a makeshift when one can no longer weep; but a writer of his early reminiscences is only trying to plumb depths in himself already established by first impressions when the initial soundings were made. He is not putting on a false face and pretending to be young.

A child who never wept till he was ten years old, would likely never weep at all. And a child of ten who had not already thought of most of the things worth writing, would never write a thing worth reading, though he lived to be a hundred.

I believe that everything centers around the philosopher in us. Yet no one can walk the narrow line of metaphysics and be happy, or even sensible. The scientist is the philosopher minus; the poet is the philosopher plus. On which side of the line will you place the child? On the side of curiosity, or the side of wonder? I am emboldened to make a brief for the poet in the child.

In my schooldays, the professions were summarized in a two-line poem:

> Rich man, poor man, beggarman, thief,
> Doctor, lawyer, Indian chief!

What a marvelous epitome for vocational guidance! Could you substitute "refrigerator salesman" in the above couplet and ever expect a boy to want to grow up?

We were educated in the hard school of wonder. We were not taught to be observant, it being assumed that we were nothing else. We were drilled with dogmas that might serve to make our observations valuable. Whatever talents appeared in us did so by reason of an inner impulse. A boy who could draw was considered an artist; a boy who could act was considered an actor; a boy who could sing was looked upon as a singer; and so on. Certain subjects were considered for most of us largely a waste of time. We had a classroom rascal, but we would have been positively frightened, not to say disappointed, to see him reform. We met in school a cross-section of what we might meet anywhere in life. You did not know whether you were sitting next to a future gangster or a future archbishop. Frankly, Sister did not know either, and that is why she was so solicitous for all of us in her prayers. I am not saying ours was the best education in all points. I am simply saying what it was.

We disliked school on the whole, and were not expected to

prefer it to our homes and holidays. Our lessons were tasks, not recreations. We did, of course, take recreation, by engaging in games in the yard during the recess periods, but we never got any marks for that. Our classrooms were not museums, playrooms, menageries. Toys were not brought in to teach us mechanics, flowers to teach us botany, nor fossils to enable us to visualize our grandparents in the jig-saw puzzle stage. Marvel and moron, we were all herded together; the bright learned lots from the stupid, and were kept by them from the nervous strain of being always in competition. Amusing incidents occurred always of their own accord; our teacher was no vaudevillian, and never told jokes. Spontaneous drama arose out of the dullness of the environment and the versatility of our own invention. Such was the incident of Alicia and the inkwell, for the telling of which it will be necessary to know that children of my day were scolded when they were bad.

Alicia was the belle of our class. I do not remember that she was pretty, for the young are no connoisseurs of physical beauty, but I do remember that she was unusual and had ingratiating airs. Alicia was fragrant, fastidious, reserved. She was always striking a posture, preserving a pose. Her parents were wealthy, and her mother dressed her with impeccable taste. She had the most radiant assortment of hair-ribbons in Essex County.

Alicia was haughty. She condescended. She even condescended to the teacher, making it seem the latter's privilege to ask her a question; and if she muffed the question, which she not infrequently did, she did it with the air of seeming superior to knowledge.

Alicia was vain, but vanity is the lightest of all venial sins, and Alicia's innocence kept it from being willful. It is probably not till twenty or thereabouts that a girl's vanity descends to deliberate tactics, making her dangerous as a débutante, wicked as a wife, pathetic as a widow. Vanity was not a fault with Alicia, it was rather an aura with which she found herself

possessed at birth, causing in herself, as in others, the surprise
and delight a peacock experiences when it spreads its fan.

The discipline of our classroom was very severe. There was
never a spot allowed on the desk, a speck of paper on the floor.
What was our consternation, therefore, one day when Alicia,
in the act of making a Cleopatrine gesture, struck a bottle of
ink with her wrist, and sent it crashing in the aisle. What! Ink
on Sister's floor!

"Who knocked that bottle of ink on the floor!" said Sister,
whose angers were known to be righteous.

There was a dead silence. Alicia stared in horror at the remnants of her recklessness: the rolling stopper, the broken glass,
the large black smudge of ink, the queer odor tincturing the
air.

Sister eyed us row by row, hoping to trap the culprit by a
stare.

Alicia's prestige, meanwhile, was in positive peril. She
straightened herself stiffly, and prepared herself in the grand
manner for a public humiliation.

"Who knocked that bottle of ink on the floor?"

"I did!" said a brave boy in the back row, raising his hand
so as to be recognized.

"Come up here!"

He went up in Alicia's stead, stood by Sister's desk, and was
given a scolding which it took Sister an unconscionably long
time to administer. To this was added a punishment lesson
which it took him hours to do at home. And finally a commis-
sion to remain after class and scrub every inch of the inked
floor with soap and water.

I sat at my desk and writhed in agony while Alicia's hero
was being court-martialed. "Oh, why didn't I think to say
what he said?" I kept repeating to myself. "Oh, why didn't I
think to say that?"

I asked my mother that night when I went home why I

didn't think to say it, seeking her aid in analyzing the lack of chivalry in my character.

"Maybe you will think to say it next time," said my mother.

But there was no next time. Though I secretly placed ink-bottle after ink-bottle in perilous positions on Alicia's desk, not from then till the day we graduated could I get her to go near one with a ten-foot pole.

ART

IT WILL BE largely among those people called philosophers that a child's thoughts will be developed. Therefore a child should admire the philosophers. Theirs may not be an adventurous voyage, but theirs is indeed a safe harbor, and one a child will never want to be out of reach of as he bobs around in his little boat. Whenever he is beyond his depths and in danger, these faithful lifeguards of logic will rush out to rescue him. And a child in the arms of a lifeguard is surely one of the most beautiful sights in the world.

It will be largely apart from those people called mystics that a child's devotions will be pursued. But he will come to learn that it is because of their prayers that he is what little he is. Therefore a child should love the mystics. Theirs is a perilous experience, but a child will no more want to uncrown a mystic of a halo than he will want to quench a lighthouse, faithful and constant, beckoning ships with treasures to come to him, winking to himself to stay where he is.

> The time has come, the walrus said,
>   To talk of many things:
> Of ships and shoes and sealing wax
>   And cabbages and kings.

Somewhere between the lifeguard and the lighthouse you will find the child at his best, without ship or shoe under him, running barefooted in the wind. It will be just at that point where the sea and land meet each other on those terms we call the shore. There the child is at once safest and most adventure-some. There he is most himself. He will imprint his footsteps on the wax of the soft beach and watch them being washed away by the wave. He will furrow with his motions the foamy ruffles of surf and watch them being absorbed by the sand. In point of importance he will think himself to be no more than a rolling pebble or a drifting seaweed. But in point of inde-pendence he will be king of all creation.

The wind on the seashore comes at you in widths and depths. It has no length. So you trap it and send it streaming through the smallest aperture you can find—your own lips pursed—and release it in the form of pure line. You whistle. And lo, you have music!

Later on when this pure line begins to surface (to paint) itself in your music lessons, you will have harmony. Still later when it begins to shape (to sculpture) itself, you will have symphony, as you discover the afternoon your mother and father bring you to hear the Boston Symphony Orchestra, just twelve miles away from Lynn. There in a large hall, with lowered lights and hundreds of people listening ever so intently, you will find that music is still music, able to triumph over any instrument that can make it. Being music it will never be able to define itself, for art cannot define anything, least of all itself. It does not know what anything is or what it is for, but simply that it is, and points to that. Its only credential is beauty (the *splendor formae* of St. Thomas). Its only excuse is delight (the *id quod visum placet*). What music is or why it is, we do not know. But *that* it is we do, because we have heard it giving such a magnificent account of itself in symphony, pitched half way between sheer silence and sheer noise—sculptured with noise by the mallet of the kettledrummer, sculptured with silence by the baton of the conductor. And yet, brought indoors and put on expensive display, music will never be more or less than the same little free whistle you made on the beach when you were running barefooted in the wind.

However, I have no intention of experimenting with childhood so as to discover the meaning of art. There are some child psychologists who enjoy doing this. They put a child in a nursery, surround him with tunes, pictures and blocks so that grown-ups may learn from his unerring reactions what are music, painting and sculpture. The compliment is enormous, but the procedure is vicious, and one that is violently protested by the child's Guardian Angel.

> Art is for childhood, not childhood for art,
>   The lesser for the greater;
> Neither is the other and they must be pried apart,
>   Sooner or later.

Fortunately the job of prying them apart was nicely done for me by the Providence of God.

In the year 1907, when I was ten years old, my father and I went to New York for a business trip. My father went for the business, and I for the trip. We had relatives there—"distant relatives" my father called them—and with them we stayed. At least I stayed while my father went—about his business.

These relatives could not get over the fact that I was their relative, for they had never seen me before. I could not get on to the fact that they were my relatives, for I had never seen them before either. They seemed afraid that at any moment I might stop being their relative, so they tried to talk me into it, even saying I looked like them. I was afraid that at any moment they might begin to be my relatives, so I tried to stare them out of the notion, inwardly denying that I looked like anyone. They spent most of the time talking, and I staring.

There is nothing so dangerous as an epidemic of cousins. Once you get infected with the idea it will begin to spread. You will end up by being related to practically everybody. Grown-ups are great ones for claiming relationship. Children are great ones for protesting it. I thought these cousins of mine were called "distant cousins" because New York was so far away from Lynn.

Across the hall from my cousins lived a young lady who was in love. She was the great subject of interest and discussion among my cousins while I was visiting them. The young lady across the hall was in love with an artist. Thinking love to be art, she went in for it all day long, and gave up all leisure. He, thinking art to be love, went in for it all day long too, and gave up all work. Mornings, noons, nights made no difference, for they had both lost all sense of time. They broke up later with a big bang, as my cousins predicted, and as was bound to be, for she expected marriage to be a perpetual court-ship and he wanted it to be an unperpetual vow.

By the very worst of luck I unstabilized this romance. My cousins had to go one morning to a funeral, and they left me in charge of the young lady across the hall. I was, for the space of a morning, on the young lady's hands and in her artist's way. So we compromised in terms of a triangle—love, art and childhood—and went out for a walk.

With my left hand in hers and my right in his, you might have met us promenading on Fifth Avenue one morning back in 1907. We looked just like a husband, a wife and a child, and were greatly admired by all who passed us. The young lady enjoyed the experience because it seemed so real. The artist was pleased because it was so make-believe. I was totally disin-terested either way, had serious distractions when passing store windows, and at times had to be forcibly dragged along.

Where did we go? To the Metropolitan Museum of Art, sent there undoubtedly by the devil. The devil can never touch love, nor art, nor childhood, but he can raise the devil with them when they enter the Metropolitan Museum of Art in the form of a triangle.

The artist was continually paying the lady compliments born of his trade. She was a picture, a song, a poem. I believe he even mentioned Helen of Troy, Venus of Milo, and Jeanie with the Light Brown Hair. The lady kept returning him tokens born less of judgment than of sheer affection. He was the equal of Rubens, Rembrandt, Raphael—in fact, on the point of surpassing them. But here was the devil to pay. She came off badly as a masterpiece and he as one of the masters, the moment we entered . . . the Metropolitan Museum of Art.

Sensing this clearly, they immediately made frantic efforts to keep up the pretense when genius and the fruits thereof threatened to destroy it. They proceeded to become totally oblivious of all the Metropolitan Museum of Art contained except themselves. I was the very first item included in this sweet forgetfulness, and I went around the place for a solid hour, totally lost.

When I found myself alone, I first made sure there was nothing there to frighten me, and found nothing. So I kept on walking and looking. None of the things I saw either surprised or interested me. I knew too little about art to be surprised at anything, and art knew too little about me to keep me interested. I simply wandered, and wondered.

> Private faces in public places
> Are wiser and nicer
> Than public faces in private places

says the poet, W. H. Auden, and he is right. But he is describing surprise and fright, not wonder. Private faces in public places are surprising: for instance, meeting your next-door neighbor in London. You say: "Why my goodness me! My

goodness gracious! Mrs. Jones! You? And of all places!"
Public faces in private places are frightening: for instance,
meeting Mahatma Gandhi in your bath. You scream!!

But when you wonder, you neither talk nor scream. You
take out of the store-house of silence one of those little soft
exclamatory syllables which are words pared down to a point,
to show you have seen the point of something. Surprise is a
love disturbed. Fright is a *thought* disturbed. But wonder is a
silence disturbed. You say: Oh! . . . Ah! . . . Say! . . .
My! . . . Gee! . . . Gosh! . . . Wow! . . . These are the
wonder words.

What did I wonder at, when I was lost in the Metropolitan
Museum of Art? Well, I wondered at a number of things in
a simple sort of way. I did not know what the pictures and
statues were about, or who had painted or carved them. I was
absorbed merely in the fact that they were there, and kept
noticing what wonderful things they did to a room simply by
being in it. For instance, the paintings made the small rooms
seem large. And the sculptures made the large rooms seem
small. This rather primitive discovery delighted me, and I
began to whistle softly to myself. The setting was now complete. For one of the three r's of aesthetics is missing in the
Metropolitan, but the music of my whistle added Rubenstein
to Rembrandt and Rodin. And my little whistle, though
smaller than any of the paintings or sculptures, easily filled
every room I entered. Music is the only art that leaves rooms
at their proper sizes.

I think it was the half-truth lurking in this absurdity that
caused me to burst into laughter (a series of silly syllables,
totally uncontrolled, the result of almost seeing too many
points at once). At any rate, the only thing that surprised and
interested me in the Metropolitan Museum of Art was what I
myself had contributed. So I laughed all the more.

But I stopped suddenly when I saw the artist and the lady
returning.

The artist came up to me angrily, seized me by the arm, and was prepared to scold me.

"Where have you been?" he said.

"Here!"

"What were you laughing at?" and his eyes filled with suspicions.

"Nothing!"

But beware of the dissyllable in direct reply. It is hesitating around the truth. The truthful answer was:

"You!"

THE POETS AND THE MYSTICS

I THINK it was good of our teachers to foster the poet in the child, rather than make a practitioner of him. Nor do I feel, as I succumb to middle age, that poetry was a bad thing, simply because it was not the best God has to offer. I know it was so much better than the lesser things children are now given in laboratories of learning, that I am not afraid to put it in its proper place in relation to that better form of knowing which the pure contemplatives enjoy.

But I will need the full maturity of my powers to show where poetry falls short of mysticism, and I need to do so precisely here in order to make a sort of celestial preparation for some further things to come. If the reader does not find this chapter very childlike in content, at least he will find it childlike in arrangement.

Poetry is another world, absolutely. When you are in it—in the throes of composition—you do not know what you eat, what you wear, what time it is, what day of the week. Some are prepared to say you are not responsible for what you do, but this cannot be admitted. Conscience is ultimately stronger than concentration.

Francis Carlin calls the poet's state one of "fixed imagina-tion." And when the imagination gets into the habit of fixing itself to beauty, it begins to fix itself to other things, worries for instance. Poets are born worriers.

I prefer a deeper explanation of the poet's misery than that offered by Francis Carlin. I think poetry is a case wherein that phase of us which was not destroyed by original sin tries to get back to its Paradisal state, and to see by simple insight in place of round-about logic. But alas, the escape is never com-plete because of the wound of original sin. The heavy fetters of iniquity hang on the wings of the mind trying to soar. And sooner or later the strain tells, and down we tumble to earth, wounded and depressed. It is an awful price to pay, as only those know who have paid it.

The reaction to the writing of poetry is terrific, and history is strewn with the wrecks of those who could not stand the pace. But the real poets have got to stand it, and that is why, next to the mystics, they are the greatest heroes in the world.

The experience of the poets and the mystics is totally differ-ent. The poets go back to Paradise. The mystics go forward to the Beatific Vision. The hardship of falling forward from Paradise is not as great as that of falling backward from the Beatific Vision. Hence, the dark night of the mystics is even worse than that of the poets.

The poets admire the mystics and praise them. The mystics do not understand the poets, but in weaker moments they envy them.

The devil hates the mystics, but he also hates the poets. He is determined that human nature shall go neither forward to the Beatific Vision nor backward to Paradise.

The mystics want the pure white light of the Divinity. The poets want it diffracted among creatures. Poets make wretched mystics, but mystics make even worse poets. Saint John of the Cross was a great mystic, but a poor poet. John Keats was a great poet, no mystic whatsoever.

Poetry is an infinitely lesser thing than mysticism, but it is greater than ordinary thought. It is also, to some extent, a vocation. No one ever asked to be a poet, nor could he wholly escape the assignment once given. The writing of poetry is not its own reward. The poets suffer, and either Heaven awaits them or they shall have had hell on both sides of the grave.

The poets work in perishable material, endeavoring to give permanent form to words, sequences and sounds. But all these babblings will be drowned one day in the music of a celestial noise. The poets know this in their deepest hearts, and yet they go on pretending not to know it. *Sunt lacrimae rerum, et mentem mortalia tangunt*, Virgil wrote; and another poet supposed he was convincing himself of a truth when he began:

> No voice is ever drowned;
> Nothing becomes a stillness that once was a sound.

What nonsense! Even a physicist could explode it. And yet what a haunting nonsense to indulge in! The poets deal in dangerous values. They are constantly trying to eternalize the temporal and make the hereafter seem like now. And they can fool us from time to time with their pleasant tricks. But the mystics refuse to be fooled. They know we have been banished from Paradise by an angel with a flaming sword.

The mystics work in the field of imperishable material, their own immortal souls. They give forms, perpetual and harmonious, to hidden masterpieces within. They are inarticulate, mostly, in this life. But when they do burst into song, their poetry will be found to be an integral part of the hosannas of The Blessed which will vibrate forever and ever.

The poets are dreadfully insincere, but they are never deceitful. "But she is in her grave, and oh, the difference to me!" sang Wordsworth of little Lucy. But after a time it did not make *much* difference. A mystic, bereaved of Lucy, would keep her as a perpetual part of his prayer, his suffering, his very life. It would *always* make a difference to him.

Yet the mystics, unlike the poets, are deceitful. I do not mean this by way of moral, but of supernatural inconsistency. If you ask the mystics how they feel, they will reply: "Excellently, thank God!" though they may be referring only to an excellent ache in the head or an excellent pain in the stomach. They appraise such things in the light of their direct relationship to God, and talk accordingly. The poet does not understand such subterfuge. If you ask him how he feels, he will answer "Rotten!" if such be the case. He knows nothing of the brave evasions of the mystics, just as he knows nothing of their unswerving loyalties.

What purpose does the poet serve in the frightening supernatural scheme of things to which we are consigned? Well, even at his worst, the poet is at least a document, illustrating, in its positive phase, the truth of original sin, proving that there was in the primal childhood of our nature a cognoscitive directness in the mind's approach to truth never wholly destroyed by the transgression of our First Parents. The poet is one of the apples left over from Paradise, which, remaining unbitten, perished by blight.

I know there are those who want to pamper the poets and send them all to Heaven as a reward for mere aesthetic skills; but these persons are chiefly those who have never known by direct experience the emptiness of poetic achievement. To the honor of the poets be it said that very few of them have surveyed themselves with such a beatific stare. The best poets know well their own limitations, and are not ashamed to be saved by humility, as Chaucer was not, who, at the hour of death, begged Our Lord to be mindful, not of the excellence of the Canterbury Tales, but of the heinousness of his own sins, and to blot these out in the gentle Christian mercies.

If there is any point in which poetry is a good preparation for mysticism, I insist that it is neither in the object sought for as such, nor in the method of seeking it. The poet is seeking for created beauty, the mystic for uncreated. The poet is perfectly helpless without the instruments of the senses and the imagination. To the mystic the senses and the imagination ultimately become hindrances, obfuscating the clear vision of God's essence.

But this much the poet and the mystic do have in common. Both look upon the object of their quest as an absolute, for which they are willing to make any and all sacrifices. The poet for the sake of his poem will starve, go sleepless, penniless, friendless, consign himself to solitude, and bravely endure the badgering, suspicion, misunderstanding which is the lot of all those who have a precious secret to hide. In brief, he practises asceticism of the extremest kind. The logic of asceticism he can see, and, conscious of its necessity in the realm of art, he is easily persuaded to admit its reasonableness in the realm of sanctification. He is sensitive also to the value of "form," and is often led into the Church by his admiration for the liturgy. And as regards the full-time contemplatives in Religious Orders, the poet may be indifferent toward them, but he is rarely if ever intolerant of them, and that is more than you can say of the common garden-variety of men, even among Catholics. Mary seated at the feet of Christ is as thoroughly convincing to the poet as Martha cooking the dinner, though there is probably nobody in the world more desperately in need of a dinner.

Fortunately for the sake of poetry, the mystical state is one to which many are called but few are chosen, and so there is no particular danger of the poets surrendering their trade in favor of a higher urge. And once God the Father gets hold of a good poet, He seems intent on keeping him, in preference to giving him the added lift that is needed for mysticism. Furthermore, the poet is one of God's best credentials, too valuable to dispense with. For if there are poets, there must be God. If there are those who can make words that fall so beautifully on our ears in time, there must be One Whose Word will reach us even more exquisitely in eternity. Therefore, God does not banish the poets, as Plato would. For God's Republic is more generous than Plato's. Others, besides the few, can enter the Kingdom of Heaven. And, short of seeing God face to face, it is something to have trapped His vestige in a rainbow or His image in the eyes of a child.

Likewise, the poet offers most stubborn resistance to the efforts of the materialists to break down the dignity of our nature and formulate it in terms of the guinea-pig. The mystic, since his is a celestial secret locked in the heart, suffers an easy dismissal by the materialist, on the score of being frustrated, inhibited, and so on. Not so the poet, who sings an open and free song for all to read. The delicacy of the spirit's tones is in it, and the materialist has no recipes for explaining this away. And so the poet, precisely because there is something in him that is of this world and something in him that is not, is one of the best defenses civilization has to protect itself against those whose education is pursued in terms of two epistemological criteria: suspicion and surmise.

Therefore, let the poets be kept, and let the mystics be kept, too, but with their differences properly noted in time, since they will be even more conspicuous in eternity.

In the pursuit of his eternity the poet has need, just as the mystic has, to go to the theology of the Church for counsel and direction. The mystics are constantly complaining that they have difficulty in finding suitable directors. They do not ask that these directors be mystics, but that they be those who have extended theology to the point where it can exercise its domain over them with understanding, rather than ridicule.

Likewise, I know of no poet who wants a poetical confessor. But he would like a confessor who at least knows of the existence of poetry, and this by way of appreciation, not condescension.

It would be well if the theologians would realize their importance as the last refuge of all of us, and with sure knowledge and generous sympathies save both mystic and poet from the horrors of private revelation.

POETRY

Now THAT POETRY has served us so patiently in unriddling the mystery of mysticism and art, it would be ungrateful of me not to pay it a few compliments for itself. I cannot do this by defining it, as I have already stated. Nor by telling how much I admire it, which I have been doing all along. I can only point it out and present it. It is sufficiently capable of introducing itself.

Poetry stands midway between philosophy and mysticism, and is at the service of both, but in itself is neither the one nor the other. Poetry is the field in which philosophy tries to become lovable. Poetry is the field in which mysticism tries to become intelligible. Truth expresses itself in poetry by way of illustration. Love expresses itself in poetry by way of symbol. Illustration is the art of the singular in universal things. Symbol is the art of the universal in singular things. Poetry is the art of illustration and symbol: the illustration of truth and the symbolization of love.

Truth lends itself to illustration reluctantly, because it thrives on exactness and is tolerant of nothing short of a perfect illustration. Love lends itself to symbol freely, because it thrives on excess, and is lenient toward any symbol that will serve it. Somewhere, ideally, there is a perfect illustration of truth. Nowhere, save arbitrarily, is there a perfect symbol of love.

The philosopher is concerned with the universal in things, and that is why he seeks the singular in illustration. The mystic is concerned with the singular in things, and that is why he seeks the universal in symbol. The philosopher is the guardian of the chastity of being, the mystic the fosterer of its charity. When being "stays at home" it is truth, and it is the philosopher's purpose to keep it at home as much as possible. When being "goes abroad" it is love, and it is the mystic's purpose to send it abroad as much as possible. The philosopher follows being when it goes abroad in the rôle of chaperone, so as to make abroad seem at home. The mystic joins being at home in the rôle of governess, so as to make at home seem abroad.

The philosophic error against God is pantheism; against the world, monism; against origin, evolution. The mystic error against God is polytheism; against the world, manichaeism; against origin, myth. The fruit of the philosophical error is scepticism. The fruit of the mystical error is superstition. The psychological escape in scepticism is stoicism. The psychological escape in superstition is neuroticism. It not infrequently happens that the evils of both sides are dumped into the field of art, and you find the poet in the form of the pantheistic polytheist, the superstitious sceptic, the stoical neurotic, in a word: the madman. Fortunately in our day he never comes much closer to literature than the "psychological novel," in which it is impossible for poetry to understand him, much less be harmed by him. Fortunately also in our day he is coming no closer to art than some form of "dadaism" or "surrealism" in which states poetry can wither him without raising an eyebrow. Let us do so.

> Though art be on vacation,
>   The studio remains;
> The well of inspiration
>   Is backing out of drains.
>
> Come, let us daub, my crazys,
>   Surrealize the thrill
> Of soapsuds on the daisies
>   And skylarks in the swill.

> Ours not to reason whether
> Surprise surpasseth wonder,
> When man hath joined together
> What God hath rent asunder.

In states worse than this, poetry must leave the artist to the alienist.

Humor is the poetry of ideas that do not match. But madness is the *philosophy* and *mysticism* of ideas that do not match, which are neither true nor good nor can even pretend to be, not even in fun.

The philosophic approach to art (the illustration of truth) is what we call Classicism. The mystical approach to art (the symbolization of love) is what we call Romanticism. Classicism is ultimately from the Greeks. Romanticism is remotely from the Romans. The hallmark of Classicism is reticence and restraint. The hallmark of Romanticism is exuberance and abandon. Classicism is suspicious of beauty; Romanticism is overtrustful of it. The danger of Classicism is prudishness. The danger of Romanticism is promiscuity. Classicism begets false virgins in the form of vestals. Romanticism begets false wives in the form of mistresses. The art of Greece perished because it starved illustration of truth. The art of Rome passed because it over-fed symbols with love. Classicism cast aside its cloak and posed in the nude. It was trying to show the body in the soul of things, and ran out of soul. Romanticism donned all raiments and went roaming in rags. It was trying to show the soul in the body of things, and ran out of body. The Age of Pericles stiffened into stone. The Middle Ages melted into paint. Art was the innocent victim in both catastrophes.

Greece gave us the athlete, bounded by a circle, with a discus frozen in his hand. Rome gave us the troubadour, divagating in the byways, with a mandolin trembling in his fingers. Greece gave us Narcissus, casual and conceited, admiring his image in a pool. Rome gave us Romeo, importunate and im-

petuous, adoring his idol in a balcony. Truth looks down, for
it is vain. Love looks up, for it is proud. Narcissus found his
image, which was really only sunlight, but he admired it and
called it himself. Romeo found his idol, which was unmistak-
ably Juliet, but he adored her and called her the moon. Illustration is truth in shadow. Symbol is love in silhouette.

> The sun begets the shadow,
>   The moon the silhouette;
> The noon is for Narcissus,
>   The night for Juliet.
>
> The image in the water,
>   The idol in the sky,
> Are opposites that alter
>   The angle of the eye.
>
> The love behind the window,
>   The truth within the wave,
> Will keep the heart unhappy
>   And make the head behave.
>
> The bridge is set for vanity,
>   The balcony for pride:—
> Beneath a man his body
>   And above a man his bride.

I have paused to compose the above lines, partly for the
respite and pleasure of my reader, partly to clarify and sum-
marize my own thought, and partly to make an ending to this
chapter, which otherwise might never have an end.

By way of one last word, I should like to call attention to
the subtle relationship that exists between poetry and verse.

Verse is not poetry. Verse is merely a suitable filament of
words strong enough to resist, yet delicate enough to take the
poetic charge. If the resultant incandescence in language is a
blending of warmth and light, then poetry has made a verse a

poem. Truth wired to the language of all illustration would fall short of poetry as does the Apologia. Love wired to the language of all symbol would fall wide of poetry as does the Apocalypse. Neither of these masterpieces requires, nor could it use, the precision of verse. Poetry is neither rhetoric nor revelation.

Poetry is truth going lovewards and love going truthwards: truth with a positive and love with a negative charge. These are the repulsions and attractions in a poet's soul which start whirling the dynamo of inspiration that generates poetry. A poet must think with the intensity of the lover and love with the accuracy of the thinker. This counter-rotation of spiritual forces when it touches language will transmute it. The only theme capable of attracting a poet is one which contains a contrariness and a compromise. It is his to see the failure in all successes and the glory in all defeats.

God is very kind to the poet at Bethlehem, letting him kneel like a listening ass and a staring ox in the presence of that complete resolution of all poetic values: a Virgin-Mother and a God-Man.

God to poets: "Unless you become as little children, you shall not enter The Kingdom of Heaven!"

Poets to God: "And unless You become a little child, You shall not get out!"

CHILDHOOD

I BEGAN this book with my first sound. I shall end it with my first silence. Now that I am nearly through with my story, let me tell its secret. It is really time for a nap anyhow, if you have been reading me continuously, so do not mind if this chapter lulls you into silence. Do not even mind if it rocks you to sleep.

When you are really asleep but think you are awake, you are in a nightmare. When you are really awake but think you are asleep, you are in a dream. Sleep may be said to define itself in terms of a nightmare. Sleep may be said to desire itself in terms of a dream. But true sleep is neither a nightmare nor a dream. It simply is, and is sleep.

When you are always asleep but think you are awake, you are a simpleton. When you are always awake but think you are asleep, you are a loon. But a child is neither a simpleton nor a loon. I learned the first lesson from a noisy adult in the city. I learned the second lesson from a quiet adolescent in the country. Poetry was my preservative in the one case, silence my preservative in the other.

When the simpleton and the loon are united in one person, you have the childhood of the madhouse, the most monstrous example of happiness in the world. If you are undergoing this double experience in terms of genius, you are some people's definition of a poet. You are William Blake, unravelling the metaphysics of a nightmare, revelling in the mysticism of a dream. If you are enjoying the experience in terms of innocence, you are Little Boy Blue. If you possess it in the form of ingenuity, you are The Wild Man of Borneo. This is the best distinction I can make among Little Boy Blue, William Blake and The Wild Man of Borneo, for those who conceive childhood, poetry and madness to be merely different phases of the same reality.

Thought was made for the head. Love was made for the heart. A sentimentalist is one who tries to love with his head. An emotionalist is one who tries to think with his heart.

> Pease porridge hot,
> Pease porridge cold,
> Pease porridge in the pot,
> Nine days old.

Sentiment and emotion are really pease porridge in the wrong pots, and a child is a stickler for getting games right, especially when the rules are put rhythmically. Hence you will find the child to be neither a sentimentalist nor an emotionalist. Sentiment fires his head with fever, as it did mine in the case of a little winged mosquito on vacation. Emotion chills his heart to ice, as it did mine in the case of a little hair-ribboned girl at school. The thinker must be cautious, but a child is the boldest of all thinkers. The lover must be bold, but a child is the shyest of all lovers. Can it be that hair-ribbons are the wings of a girl, and wings the hair-ribbons of a gnat? No one would think so, really. No one would want them to be, really. But a poet would say they were, to the single applause of the child.

I have balanced the child with the philosopher and found him to be the poet who soared into Heaven. I have balanced the poet with the mystic and found him to be the child who fell back to earth. I have balanced the child with the artist and found him to be lost in the labyrinth of his own ubiquity. What is this earthliness of heavenly things and heavenliness of earthly things, which is constantly being lost and found, and in which poetry and childhood unite? We all know what childhood and poetry are in terms of performance. But what are they in terms of essence and idea? The answer is: "Nobody knows, and nobody cares," least of all poetry and childhood. Neither knows *what* it is nor *why* it is, but simply *that* it is, and it is enough.

The perfect recollection of self in remembrance is silence. The perfect recollection of self in forgetfulness is sleep. In this sense poetry is silence. And in this sense childhood is sleep.

You never have childhood completely, even when you hold it in your arms. You never lose it completely, even when you send it abroad to play. The same is true of poetry. Poetry will come to you when you least expect it, and will go from you when you want it most. The same is true of childhood. Both

are impervious to analysis and synthesis, the analysis of ratioc-
ination and the synthesis of rapture.

> They draw no conclusions,
> And make no resolutions.

How then can you get them to behave—I mean in the
sphere of their clear and especial duties. It cannot be done by
petting them. Parents try petting their children and patrons
try petting their poets, but there is in both childhood and
poetry an essential chastity that resists all excess in affection.
Neither can it be done by scolding them, as preceptors do
with children and critics with poets. For both childhood and
poetry have a charity that forgives and disregards all excess in
correction. Frankly, childhood and poetry are both imps,
amenable to no motives except reward and punishment.
Frankly, you must either bribe or scare them. Ultimately you
will need both Heaven and Hell to be effective. For Heaven
is the poetry of bribe, and Hell the childhood of scare.

Are poetry and childhood the same thing? I do not know,
neither does anyone. If they are one, then they will never
know how to divide, for their essence is in simplicity. If they
are two, then they will never know how to unite, for their
uniqueness is in distinction. But this much I do know: there
are no two things about which it is possible to say so many
same things as about poetry and childhood—unless they be
silence and sleep. And the importance of silence to sleep is the
importance of poetry to childhood.

Every little boy is enough of a poet to imagine he is the
general of his soldiers. Every little girl is enough of a poet to
fancy she is the mother of her dolls. Now a shortage of soldiers
and a shortage of babies might be responsible for a world collapse. And wouldn't it be awful if the soldiers started killing
off the babies in an effort to put things right again?

> Humpty Dumpty sat on a wall.
> Humpty Dumpty had a great fall.
> All the king's horses and all the king's men
> Couldn't put Humpty Dumpty together again.

And who is Humpty Dumpty? He is an egg on a wall: poetry's symbol for all things unborn.

A child turns his playthings into thoughts. It is the only way he can learn. A poet turns his thoughts into playthings. It is the only way he can teach. The education of the child is in the playthings of the world, and the instruction of the world is in the playthings of the poets. So, the nursery never ceases and life is forever a game.

Armed with such wisdom one might conquer the world. Armed with such wisdom one does. All things fall swiftly into place when you are playing a game.

> Rockaby baby, on the tree top—
> When the wind blows the cradle will rock,
> When the bough breaks the cradle will fall,
> And down will come baby, cradle and all!

Incidentally, I might mention that the "all" in the impending catastrophe of the last line in the above ditty includes not only childhood, but also poetry, silence and sleep.

Now as far as there can be a definition, Rockaby Baby is a perfect definition of both poetry and childhood. Of course no philosopher will accept it, for he wants it in terms of a syllogism which he can share with others. Of course no mystic will accept it, for he wants it in terms of a hieroglyphic which only he can decipher. M. Maritain in his *Art et Scolastique* tries to turn poetry into prudence, so it can be passed around among the metaphysicians. Abbé Bremond in his *Prière et Poésie* attempts to turn poetry into prayer, so it can be whispered to a few mystics. But poetry will not be laicized or clericalized by these easy snares. I cannot think of a more imprudent place to put Rockaby Baby than on a tree top, yet that is where poetry puts him and the child likes it. I cannot think of a more unprayerful thing to say to Rockaby Baby than to remind him of the pleasures of infanticide. Yet poetry does and the child thinks it is grand. Prudence is an excellent thing, and so is prayer. But whatever else poets and children are, they are not *pious prudes*.

I am willing to sway with Rockaby Baby on the tree top in a perfect statement of what poetry is. If the bough breaks and the cradle falls, then down will come baby, cradle, and the author of this book. But they will not, and I shall show why.

The to and fro of sound is a lullaby. The to and fro of motion is a rockaby. The to and fro of music is a melody. The to and fro of words is a poem. The to and fro of thought is beauty. The to and fro of expression is art. The to and fro of silence is sleep.

> The vanity of water is a fountain,
> The vanity of land is a mountain:
> The modesty of wet is a well,
> The modesty of dry is a dell.

And what are vanity and modesty but the to and fro of some lovely thing that deserves to be admired? But let us go back to Rockaby Baby.

The to and fro of water is a wave. The to and fro of air is a breeze. The to and fro of sky is a cloud. The to and fro of light is a star. Look out! We are rocking too hard! The bough is about to break and the cradle fall, not downwards, but upwards, into the infinite spaces! . . . *The to and fro of God is a Child!*

Far beyond the tree top . . . far beyond the stars, those occasional clarities of the philosophers . . . far beyond the background of the sky into which the mystics perpetually stare . . . tucked in the nursery of The Divinity—in the great silence of God, in an eternal sleep which is neither a nightmare nor a dream, but the living ecstasy of The Blessed Trinity—there is a *Filius Unigenitus*: an Only Begotten Child, who is the to and fro of The Father and The Holy Ghost, everlastingly rockabied and lullabied in the sacred processions of The Godhead.

THE EXILE

ON ANY DAY but Saturday—and for our sakes not on Sunday—but with haunting regularity on five days of the week you could hear his call in our street. He was whiskered and hunchbacked and wore a long-tailed coat and an over-sized hat that slid over his ears. He drove a loose-wheeled wagon that seemed to be rolling all ways at once and was drawn by a horse that had not been currycombed for months. The horse looked more stuffed than real, and there were times when so did the driver. Taken together they seemed an epitome of lazy motion, yet they were models of persistence in faithfully returning for the errand which brought them to our street. The boys pelted the man with bad fruit and called him vile names. He never answered them, except to go on shouting in a monosyllable the purpose for which he had come.

I was eleven years old when there suddenly dawned on me the tragedy of this poor vagabond's existence. True, I had never joined with the hoodlums in stoning or abusing him, but I had failed to appreciate the extent to which he was a victim rather than an enemy. When this realization came to me, I decided to let him know how I felt toward him by offering a few cheery words of sympathy. These he disdained as something suspicious. He merely rubbed his long beard and drove on. His refusal to be pitied made me all the more interested in his desolation, so I determined to follow him, discover his origins, find out where he lived. This I did during one of the summer holidays. I shadowed him for a whole day, even going without lunch at noon. I trailed him to the waterfront, and under the bridge, and down several side streets, and into a slum of sorts. I saw him unhitch his wagon and leave it standing in a yard. I saw him put his horse to feed in a shed, and then mop his brow wearily, and enter his house for supper. It was just at the hour of sunset. The insults of the day were over. He had a wife, so I discovered, and she was preparing his evening meal. And he had a daughter.

There she sat on the door-step, in the midst of her own, a dark Madonna of seventeen, waiting for the waters of Baptism to fulfil in her eyes the New Testament promised by the Old, and to which she had far more title than any of us Irish and Italian interlopers who mingle the Faith with fun.

She was reading a book when I first saw her. Eyes are never so lovely as when they are avoiding your own. Later I saw her rise and carry a basket on her head, and move among her kind as one destined for election and sacrifice. Her tribe sensed this in her, and that is why she dared not, save in ambush, talk to a Christian, even to a Christian child.

The incident left me speechless, and it was not until years later that I knew what I had wanted to say—not on my own account, for such loves are purely literary—but as hostage for someone who would be songless in her bereavement. Here is what I wrote, finally:

> In your dark eyes I see is so,
> Something I needed lots to know.
>
> Something Isaiah said I find
> Now makes a meaning in my mind.
>
> What Judith, Ruth and Esther were,
> For the first time I now infer.

> Our Lady's voice unto my ear
> Becomes more definite and dear.
>
> Rarest, the world is all awry,
> But father, mother, you and I
>
> Will quadrilaterally allied
> Defeat the death we shall have died
>
> When . . .

and I dared not add the last line, which would be prophetic of her destiny.

"But where shall I go?" she said after her Christening, which was undertaken at peril of her life, even over attempts to poison her food.

"For contemplation, warm countries are best," she was told.

"Will South America do?"

"It will do."

"Is it far enough?"

"Not quite far enough, but it will do."

"And there can be no attachments?"

"In your case, none. For you the price of God is everything else. You must make a supernatural equivalent of what is native in you: 'an eye for an eye, and a tooth for a tooth.' "

"What about my prayers?"

"It were better to be free even in your prayers. Let Christ choose your favorites. Remember, you are of His blood, even before it was poured on the Cross. There are cheap attachments one can make to creatures under guise of offering novenas in their behalf. Yours must be a sword renouncement, like Abraham's with Isaac!"

"Can't you put it more gently than that?"

"There is no way of putting it more gently than that."

But there was, and I was determined to find it, even though it might take me years. For it is the business of the poets to be

the servants of the mystics, to catch their cast-off thoughts,
and to phrase their farewells. Even a martyrdom is softened
when it is set forth in song. That a strong song was needed, I
could clearly see, one equal to the mettle of the maid.

Because of the girl in the Gospel who lost her groat,
Because of the little boy by the fountain who lost his boat,
Because of the nervous piccolo player who lost his note—

Because there are partings on earth too hard to be had:
The waving wench on the dock and the land-loosed lad,
The widow, the warden, the jail, and the son gone mad—

We two who were sentenced on earth to be braver far
Than any except what Our Lord and Our Lady are,
Shall singly shine henceforth, as a star and a star;

And not interfere any more with each other's light,
No matter how murky the mist, how dismal the night,
Or whether the clouds conceal or reveal us right.

Now, mind you, I do not want you even to pray for me.
Let our dismissal be done in a downright way for me,
And neither be sad about it, and neither be gay for me.

For nothing can grieve for nothing, is that not true?
And nothing plus nothing is nothing, not one nor two,
And you willed to know me as nothing, and I willed you.

And God will be pleased, if God can be pleased at all,
As we raise between us the sky and the high sea-wall,
So to slake our souls in the wastes where His pities fall.

   She sailed to South America on a small boat. The boat
weighed only five thousand tons. I was on the dock, pretending to be one of the baggage boys, looking among the visitors
for him who would miss her most. But I could find no one
bidding her farewell.

I watched the ship till it reached the crest of the horizon, and sank in the far southeast.

Only two corollaries on this subject remain in my notes, a sestet and a double quatrain, on an identical theme. It is a difficult theme to handle, and I often laugh at my efforts, for they are perfectly contradictory.

The first:

> I must regret my partings more,
>   Renounce, not just refuse,
> And make a face, and pace the floor,
>   And burst into boo-hoos,
> When someone ambles out the door,
>   I am so pleased to lose.

The last:

> What soared into the sun
>   Will return one day,
> Remolded and respun
>   In a rarer ray;
>
> Identical, yet different,
>   Indeed, Divine;
> And what was never, never meant
>   For me, will be mine!

THE IMAGINATION GUY

IT IS NOT OFTEN you can stare into a person's eyes without causing embarrassment, but you could with the Imagination Guy. And the reason was because he saw you only in a blur. You were less than a silhouette to him when you entered his room. You were perpetually prismed with the wrong colors, shrouded in a haze, covered with a cloud around the edges of which would come floating the sound of your voice:

"Good morning!"

"That you, kid?"

"Yes."

"Come in and sit down and tell me how you are."

"I'm fine."

"That's the ticket!"

Then he would inquire if there was a morning paper in the hall. And I would go and find that there was. Mrs. Hasenfus, his landlady, was usually making beds when I arrived, and she was glad to have someone take the Imagination Guy off her hands and entertain him until her chores were finished. He wore a bathrobe and slippers and sat in a comfortable chair. He usually remained undressed and unshaved until noon. His hair was grey, and he had a tooth missing here and there. He was in his middle fifties when I knew him.

I would return with the morning paper and seat myself in a chair opposite his.

Cataracts—that's what the doctor said the Imagination Guy had in his eyes. Cataracts! I was always peering into his eyes intently whenever they were wide open so as to find the little Niagara Falls I supposed were flowing in each retina. But he would invariably blink at the wrong moment and spoil the experiment.

"Mind reading me the headlines?" he would say when he heard me rumpling the newspaper, while he fumbled for a cigarette and lit it.

"I'll be glad to!" I would say. And I would unfold the paper and begin to read the largest words printed on the front page.

PLANS FOR ELEVATED GRADE-CROSSING COMPLETED. WORK ON CENTRAL SQUARE STRUCTURE TO BEGIN AT ONCE.

That was enough when you were reading to the Imagination Guy. You might then lay down the paper for a while and listen to him talk. That nimble brain of his would immediately begin to anticipate the story and tell it far better than it was written in the news.

"It's about time they got going on that thing," he would say, as he visualized the whole construction with closed eyes. "There's been an average of twelve people killed down there every year as far back as I can remember. Imagine having a railroad running right through the main street of your city! And we're supposed to be up-to-date! That's the worst of living in a town that was founded in sixteen hundred and twenty-nine. Never seems to want to grow up, if you know what I mean. Gets cluttered up with a lot of old fossils who want to impede our progress. I don't expect anyone has been able to keep track of the number injured down at that crossing. I nearly got knocked off myself once. It was when the gates were down and I didn't hear the gong ringing. Pretty hard for anyone to hear it ringing with all the racket and noise and the jangling of the street cars. I expect this new plan will cost a lot of money. Three or four hundred thousand dollars, I should imagine. But it's worth it. They're going to have a lot of trouble, though, enlarging the street. There's Tobey's tobacco store. That's got to go. And I expect it will cut into Emerson's lunch room. And I imagine it will block off a lot of light in some of the shops. You won't be able to see yourself in Hooley's bar. Then I'm afraid those pillars that hold up the tracks will cause a lot of trouble. With automobiles coming along at the rate they are, there'll be a lot of them bumping right into those pillars. However, I'd rather bump into something than have it bump into me. And it's a crêpe and an undertaker sure, kid, if you ever get bumped by a railroad train . . ."

I used to sit in absolute amazement at the way the Imagination Guy could develop in soliloquy the barest suggestions from the headlines in the daily news. He seemed to have all Lynn tucked in his head, its lay-out, its inhabitants, its history.

"You're a wonder!" I would say to him.

"Who?"

"You!"

"Why?"

"The way you remember everything. The way you imagine everything. The way you *see* everything with those cataracts in your eyes."

"Aw, forget it!" he would say in a depreciative snarl. "After all, I've got nothing else to do. . . . But how about turning to the sports page and reading me about yesterday's ball games."

The lingo of the sports page is the most fantastic in the world. And it is all condensed like cream in the headlines. Centuries from now, when the English language has perished, I wonder if some scholiast of the future will be able to decipher one iota of meaning if he has at hand only the leaders from an American sports page. Yet there were nine innings' worth of rapturous instruction and entertainment in every one of these phrases as I read them out loud to the Imagination Guy:

MARANVILLE'S BUNT SAVES HAVERHILL. . . . TIGERS CLAW HOSE FOR SIXTH STRAIGHT. . . . PIRATES SINK REDS IN NINTH FRAME. . . . CARRIGAN'S PEG NIPS GEORGIA PEACH OFF SECOND. . . . CUBS RESCUED BY TINKER TO EVERS TO CHANCE.

Friendship with the Imagination Guy implied obligations as well as privileges. For it seemed that every place you went you should be storing up things you had noticed and liked, so as to be able to tell them to him on your return. I might have remained his scout for years were it not for the following incident.

"Been swimming?" he said one day when I returned from a dip in the ocean.

"Yes."

"How was the water?"

"Cold."

"I mean how did it look?"

"Same as always."

"Was it blue or green?"

That stopped me.

"Don't you know the difference between blue water and green water?"

"No."

"Well, when it's calm and the wind is down and there's no storm brewing, the water is blue. It's just like a mirror, and takes it color partly from the sky. But when the wind is up and it's rough and a storm is threatening, it gets restless, frantic, green, ready to leap up in high waves!"

"I never noticed that."

"Well, you ought to. For pity's sake, don't let that beach get wasted on you, kid. We've got the most beautiful beach on the Atlantic Coast. King's Beach! There's nothing like it from Maine to Florida. Ever notice how Dow's Rock extends out on one side and Red Rock on the other, taking a large armful of ocean and hugging it right to our shore? The Bay of Naples has nothing on our little bay, I'll tell you. And haven't we got our own Egg Rock out in the distance, pretending it's Vesuvius? I love every inch of sand on that beach, and all the little pebbles. I love the small boats anchored off the point, bobbing up and down in the tide. I even love the sand pails and toy shovels of the children, and the colored umbrellas that shade the ladies when they bring their families down there for a day's outing."

I paused long enough to allow this rapture to dissipate. And then I glared at him with a rebellious look in my eye.

"Now see here!" I said, "I was the one who went swimming today, not you! And King's Beach isn't nearly as lovely as you say it is. Nothing is as lovely as you say it is. You make things lovely by the way you think about them and talk about them. No wonder they call you the Imagination Guy!"

He smiled a disappointed smile, showing all the vacancies in his teeth. He realized he had lost his hold on me. He dropped his head and sighed.

"I see you're on to me," he said.

"Doesn't everyone get on to you after a while?"

"Shhhh! Here comes the landlady!"

THE CLASSICS

IT IS STRANGE that I remember the days of my middle childhood—that is the years from seven till fourteen—better than I do the period of the next four years that followed. The Jesuits were responsible for that.

At the age of thirteen I was taken from the charge of the nuns, and sent to Boston to be educated by the Jesuits. It was a most fortunate choice on the part of my parents.

I was just at an age when a vivid fancy and an undisciplined fondness for day-dreaming were ready to roam for no serious purposes, and deserved to be checked. It was the precise time when the essential intellect, in itself and for itself, needed to be given something substantial to do: to stop amusing itself by way of reverie, and to be informed with the habit of reflection.

Up till fourteen, a boy's imagination is as aimless as a butterfly, and it is best to let him browse through books as he pleases, rather than harness him with commands to read only what is important in literature. Up till fourteen a boy is too sensitive to be in charge of anyone save a woman. Up till fourteen the psychological differences between a boy and a girl are so slight that they often thrive on the same stories and play the same games.

But at fourteen, a boy's world changes. Henceforth he must

set his face toward the life ahead with a military outlook and a soldier's reserve. Co-education after fourteen is a farce. There is a world for woman and a world for man, and you will confound the two at your peril.

I got a head start on the critical age by one year.

The Jesuits, though soldiers, did not put uniforms on us or give us guns to carry. The Jesuits, though psychologists, did not outline for us through biological charts and graphs the emotional evolution through which we were passing. The Jesuits plunged us into the classics.

It was well enough to think, but did you know what you were thinking and why you were thinking it? And had you noticed, in your blank moments, the frightening dependence that must exist between thinking something and expressing it?

"Let us take thought out of the mould of language in which you are now using it," said the Jesuits, "and recast it in another mould, so as to show you exactly what its face value is. Let us choose as a medium of expression that used by men at the highest points of culture in the world's history, the civilizations of Greece and Rome. You are young American boys employing a hybrid, uninflected language, bristling with so many and such diverse rules that not even a professional grammarian knows them all, a language completely dissociated from its origins and all but unintelligible in its etymology save to the most meticulous savants. Is that a nice language for a boy to learn how to think in? No, not if there is a better at hand. And there is!"

"We will teach you," said the Jesuits, "the two most beautifully ordered and inflected languages in the history of the world. Let us see you try out your thoughts in those languages! You may have them as rich and pure and free from mongrel importations as little boys once received them in ancient Greece and Rome. Then you will know what is worth saying, and how best to say it, from having first learned what needed to be said at all. And it will fill your life with purpose.

And you will begin to be refined little gentlemen. And you will always know what to do."

We began with Latin grammar, and had hardly got on to the syntax and vocabulary of that, when it was followed by Greek grammar. We began to study the by-paths and delicate detours of human thought in such matters as intention, purpose, result, causality, wish, surmise, exhortation and command. We learned the "moods" that could affect a statement by reason of indicative, infinitive, subjunctive and optative colorings. We took sentences apart and studied their complexity, dependence, and the various ways in which an idea or phrase could be qualified. We watched a single word alter its ending as it went from nominative to genitive, to dative, to accusative case, always letting you know *what it was* by its root formation, and *what it was doing* by its variable syllable. In no time we were reading the letters of Cicero, listening to the stories of Herodotus, surveying in a virginal, poetic vision, the whole of life with Homer.

What with themes, tasks, exercises, memory assignments, translations, parsing—the Jesuits left you time for little else in life besides your lessons. One would almost say they allowed you as few distractions as an angel. You took language completely apart, and reformed it with the graces of personal choice. It was the birth in you of what is known as "style."

In a short time you found that you were thinking differently from other boys in your neighborhood, more fundamentally, with more care in your statements, more maturity and sureness in your judgments. You could detect fallacies in what others had to say, and were inwardly censoring what you had to express yourself. Other boys noticed this in you, and either avoided you as one above them, or else came to you for advice. There might be a tendency in this training to make one a snob, but a touch of snobbery in a boy, like a touch of vanity in a girl, is not necessarily dangerous, and often the foundation of future greatness.

Back, back, back you went with the Jesuits, through the history of Western Civilization, back through the Middle Ages, back to the times of the Roman Emperors, even back to the Greek gods and the twilight of mythology. Civilization became the most important word in your vocabulary. And little by little you began to be civilized, to differentiate what was of the spirit and what of the senses, what was trivial and what important, what was ephemeral in man and what never changed.

The Jesuits put no premium on your being clever, only on your being intelligent, and on your ability to give reasons for what you thought and said. They weaned you away from a world, then known as Lewis Carroll's, and now as Walt Disney's, and drove you to an admiration for the Roman valor and the Greek restraint. You were able literally to *trace* thought, classical and purposeful, in the outlines of the Doric, Ionic and Corinthian columns. Imaginary figures derived from abstractions began to people your mind: Minerva and her wisdom, Ceres and her fruitfulness, Juno and her righteousness. Thought came first with the Jesuits, and symbols second, reversing the order of the kindergarten. Illustration followed the values established by essential reason. The day of the picturebook had passed. The day of the dry text had begun. Mother Goose had flown off on a broomstick, never to return. Santa Claus had at last died in the frozen north.

"If you send your boy to school to a slave," so runs an old Greek proverb, "he will become a slave!"

If you send him to school to a Jesuit, will he become a Jesuit?

It so happens, sometimes.

FAREWELL WITHOUT TEARS

WHEN ONE is seated in a dentist's chair, with one's mouth full of dentist's fingers and dentist's instruments, it is difficult to hold a conversation. One becomes all yawn, and the only word it would seem possible to pronounce is the name of the town in the Tyrol where they put on the Passion Play.

"How old are you?" said the dentist, while he elongated my mouth to suit his convenience.

"Oberammergau!" I replied.

"What!" he exclaimed, withdrawing all his tools at once.

"Seventeen!" I answered clearly, as I rinsed my throat with water and spat into a little silver whirlpool on the arm of the chair.

"That third tooth from the front never came down, I see. It's embedded in the gum. I'd give it a few more years though. It may grow down yet!"

"Thanks."

I rose from my chair, paid him his bill, and bade him adieu.

"What's this I hear about you?" the dentist said, as I was getting my hat.

"It's true," I replied. "That's why I came to have my teeth examined."

"Well, good luck!"

"Thanks."

Then I went to the doctor's for a more protracted investigation.

"What's this I hear about you?" said the doctor.

"It's true."

"You're young."

"I'm seventeen!'

"Are you sure you know your own mind?"

"I think so," I said, expanding my chest. "But how about my physical condition?"

He examined me a long time, required me to remove my shirt and take many deep breaths, and then said: "You're fit!"

"Good-bye, doctor!"

"Good-bye!"

Then there was the clothier's to go to for a couple of black suits. And the shoe store for extra pairs of shoes. And the haberdasher's for shirts, stockings and linen. And the parish rectory for my Baptismal certificate. And the baggage store for a trunk. And, oh yes!, to the men's furnishings shop for an umbrella.

It was my first unborrowed umbrella.

I was about three weeks in getting everything I needed.

Finally, all washed, dressed and packed, I stood one day at the top of our front stairs, ready to knock on the door of my mother's room.

Good God, what was I doing? Was this the result of a classical education? Or is there a sense in which a boy does not know his own mind?

I knocked on my mother's door.

She was dressed in bright colors, endeavoring to please me.

She kissed me one, twice, a dozen times, saying nothing.

My father, speaking for both of them, embraced me and said: "Good-bye, dear!"

My little brothers looked unhappy, and my little sister wept and would not be consoled with a million kisses.

I took a last look at all the rooms in our home. A last look at our neighbors' houses, and the traffic going to and fro in the street. A last look at our lawn and our lovely verandah. A last look at the number on our front door. A last look at the beaches below us, where I used to swim.

The by-gone beaches and limbs of brown,
When hoops were rolling around the town,
And London Bridges were falling down!

The car was ready, and my belongings packed in the rear.
The gears shifted, and we were off.

The next day I was in New York. It was September 7, 1914.
I received Holy Communion at the Church of St. Francis
Xavier. I ate breakfast in an automat lunch. I took a walk on
Riverside Drive and visited Grant's Tomb.

At noon I took the boat that sails up the Hudson.

I arrived in Poughkeepsie at five-thirty.

A short auto ride brought me to the Novitiate of St.
Andrew-on-Hudson, the training school for young Jesuits in
the Eastern States. It was just six o'clock, Angelus time, on
the Eve of Our Lady's Nativity.

We were fourteen novices entering on that day, and pretty
raw recruits we were, and looked, even to each other. We
were first brought to the chapel to say a prayer. Then we
went to the dormitories and were shown the hard beds on
which we were to sleep. Then to the cubby-holes where we
were to put our clothes. Then to the washrooms, where each
was given a small wash-bowl for himself, with one spigot in it,
spouting a stream of icy cold water. I had brought a safety
razor, and my first blade lasted me two years, and my first
cake of shaving soap, four.

We were taken to the refectory for supper.

After supper we were brought to the Master of Novices for
a first inspection. We entered his room individually. He was
a short, slight man, about five feet, two inches in height, and
weighed not more than a hundred pounds. His name, appro-
priately, was Father Pettit. He was *little* Father Pettit to us all
from then until he died. And it was not I who coined him the
adjective.

This is the story of what I chose to be at the age of seventeen, and exactly the story of what I would want to be again, were the choice once more to be mine.

But I forgot to tell what the Jesuit Master of Novices said to me when I visited him that first night in his room.

"I see you have a tooth missing!" he said. "We'll have to have that fixed!"

THE FIRST COMMAND

THERE is a great heritage bequeathed to aspirants in all Religious Orders by their spiritual forebears. It is the First Command.

There are copious rules developing around this initial order of obedience, but nothing can be attempted in the ascetical life until it has been established. You do not find it placarded in the cloister corridors as you do in a busy office or a hospital. It is the essential atmosphere into which you move, and you either accept it as sacred, or else profane it with every unnecessary sound of your voice.

The First Command can be issued in a single word, the most thunderous in the world when shouted. Birds begin to twitter when it settles in the air. It is the cricket's opportunity and the dove's delight. In it you can hear the leaves crinkling on the trees, the leaves turning in the books. It is the language of resignation, patience, forgiveness of injuries. Beethoven utilized it to compose the world's great symphonies. Christ hid in it for thirty years, preparing Himself for His mission. It is all that is audible of the planets circling the sun, of buds growing in the field.

In fulfillment of the First Command one notices the time passing, knows that it is time, knows that it is not eternity.

"There cannot be two hundred men in this house! It is impossible! Where is everyone? I hear nothing! What are they all doing?"

Recreations were merrier because of the observance I mention. A bell would ring and a burst of voices be heard, anxious to tell the happy thoughts that had been saved up during the day. A bell would ring again. Sociability ceased instantly and all reverted to the call of the First Command.

When you had any of what was offered you by the First Command you had all of it at once, and each had it all to himself. It was measureless and immeasureable, wider than the ocean and as large as God.

They were building an artesian well at St. Andrew and I used to count the strokes of the heavy drill plunging in the rock. I figured that it would strike a hundred and seventeen thousand times in a month.

I have seen two ascetories filled with novices kneeling for solid hours and hours of prayer in perfect tableau.

Some could not stand the monotony imposed by the First Command, and they packed their trunks and returned home to their mothers.

But on it went after their departure, the inexorable rule of the Religious, which when he forgets he figuratively tears down the walls of the cloister and shatters the great pillars of peace.

The First Command brought the uninitiated to the edges of the spiritual desert where alone the voice of God is to be heard. Yet there were moments of bewilderment when you had so much of it on your hands you knew not what to do. You drew little circles on paper with a pencil; you plucked blades of grass; you examined the bark on trees; you counted ants scampering into the little holes in their hills.